WE ARE ALL IN THIS TOGETHER

Holistic Approach on Immigration and Psychology

SANDRA FERREIRA

outskirtspress

DENVER, COLORADO

Outskirts Press, Inc.
http://www.outskirtspress.com

ISBN: 978-1-4787-6935-4

Outskirts Press and the "OP" logo are trademarks belonging to Outskirts Press, Inc.

DEDICATION

Dedicated to the memory of my dear father, Antonio, the first of four generations of immigrants before me, and to all my dearest ancestor immigrants from various parts of the world, since the beginning of time.

I am especially grateful for the contribution of Pastor Gerson Anunciação for the numerous meetings and long conversations about his experience working with the Brazilian immigrant community in America.

CONTENTS

INTRODUCTION

Immigration is an ancient phenomenon, which started in prehistoric eras. Throughout human history, migration has taken different characteristics and gained new meanings, according to the social, political, and economic realities prevailing in each place and era.

Nowadays, relationships of power and domination have become very complex, thanks to the expansion of territories and the concentration of power in the hands of the few, determined primarily by economic factors.

We will focus on the issues of immigration in the USA; however, such issues need to be understood in the context of the history of humanity as well as the context of today's world. Many migrate to the USA from all over the world in search of the so-called "American Dream". For some, this dream translates to a life of freedom; for others, financial progress; for others, safety, away from political or religious persecution or war. However, the reality in many cases ends up revealing itself as quite distant from the desired goal, and can be best described as a nightmare rather than a dream. Even for those whose goals are achieved, the immigration process is always permeated by variable doses of pain, suffering, and loss for the first-generation immigrant.

This book is intended to bring into focus the issues, conflicts, conquests, and losses of immigrants of various origins, mainly Brazilians, taking into consideration their ethnological differences from American culture, and the aspects involved in this adaptation. It also has the objective to raise awareness and to promote a broader and deeper reflection on the reality of the migratory phenomenon in America and in the world.

Such understanding correlates first-world countries' political and economical interests in so-called globalization to the migration phenomena of the present day. It also promotes a deeper reflection on the psychological impact and oppressive processes related to cultural shock, discrimination, and acculturation of the immigrant individual, as of the comprehension of their position as victims of the 20th- and 21st-centuries' social, political, and economic systems.

We will mention some of those theories and concepts, based on their current definitions in social and intercultural psychology, dedicated to the studies of the multicultural phenomena, having as a reference case studies of immigrants interviewed or treated by me through psychological counseling, as well as my own experience as a Brazilian immigrant in the USA.

The described cases are real; however, the individuals' names and personal data are altered to preserve their identity and privacy.

The motivation for such work came from observing the constant patterns of symptoms, difficulties, and experiences of discrimination and oppression suffered by immigrants, consistent with the data published on studies on acculturation and social psychology. The clinical cases observed were accumulated through twenty-five years of clinical psychology experience in private practice, as well as my own experience as a Brazilian immigrant, naturalized and residing in the United States for almost seventeen years.

During all my years in America, I have been working as a psychotherapist, seeing patients from different ethnicities, and previously I have done the same for over ten years as a psychologist in Brazil.

Some of the personal experiences are described in Part II of this book and have the sole purpose of validating the impact of cultural shock in the immigrant's life, as of the reality of the discrimination phenomena of the minorities in America, deepening the understanding of the suffering of the immigrant individuals in general, in order to bring to surface the underground of the discriminatory reality, which is not so well perceived and understood by the American and the world citizen who has never experienced residence in another country. The immigrant him/herself, despite experiencing such reality, has little or no awareness and understanding of it as well, or the collective factors associated with his or her own personal experience and needs, or even of their correlations to his or her psychological conflicts and the global phenomena.

Therefore, I wish to emphasize the collective constructive agenda behind this work, to help to understand not only the Brazilian immigrant community, but our world and reality, as a human race, in relation to the immigration phenomenon. I can guarantee with conviction the absence of any personal resentments, complaints, and especially any aversion to the USA as a nation, which now I consider my own country. On the contrary, by considering myself privileged in my life opportunities both here and in my country of origin, Brazil, regardless of the differences and adjustments suffered through my journey here as an immigrant, I feel the RESPONSIBILITY to contribute to the collective growth of America, and consequently the world, as the immigration phenomenon affects the whole nation on many levels, and is interlaced with the reality of our species on this planet.

Knowing that awareness of every problem is the first step to its solution, we need to reflect and understand in a more consistent, wider and deeper way, as a global and trans-historical phenomenon, instead of seeing it minimalisticaly as a local and superficial issue, in which the countries that receive large waves of immigrants are victims and the immigrants the villains, transgressors of the law, even when they come through legal means, as they are perceived as competitors and narrowers of opportunities for local citizens. In reality, we are all somehow victims, native people and immigrants, whites and blacks, religious and atheists individually and collectively of a predatory economy in which only 1% of the population retains the economical and political power. The economic oligarchy, maintaining the intention of endless expansion, destroys the middle and lower classes and compromises the existence and stability of the whole nation and planet, destroying local economies and eco-systemic equilibrium, by reaching global frontiers through globalization tools.

It is also pertinent to mention that the immigration phenomenon and its related problems is not a problem exclusive to America. The social-political-economic exploitation of individuals and people is recurrent throughout the history of humanity since the begining of time. In actuality, domination, competition, and disputes for territory can be noticed even among animals in nature. The biggest difference is that their motives are restricted to their survival and the survival of their species and do not risk the balance of the eco-system. Humanity, on the other hand, lost with time the concept of collectiveness, community, and interdependence among people and with nature. The cognitive and technological development of *Homo sapiens* these days leads us to the folly of ignoring the basic and essential knowledge that we are part of and dependent on our natural environment, and on our interdependence with each other as social beings. This balance between our species and nature is absolutely essential to the existence of our planet, and therefore to our own survival as species. We lost the basic notion that our species cannot exist without nature, as there is no individual existence without the collective. The temporary gains through domination, oppression, and destruction of one another and nature bring inevitable outcomes of self-destruction to all of us, without exception. Such practices and values are, therefore, representative of regression and throwbacks instead of evolution, by forgetting basic knowledge learned long before we became "sapiens."

Part one consists of synopses and reflections on existing studies, public official data from American government websites, knowledges on the subject of immigration psychology, and history of immigration along with a few samples of clinical cases. Part two consists on memoirs and reflections related to the immigration phenomenon.

The studies of immigrants also present the large distance between nature, characteristics and behavior of the immigrant of any ethnicity, living outside of his or her country and his or her correspondent lives in his or her country of origin. Their habits, behavior, health status and even intelectual performances need to be understood and considered under the prism of the acculturation process, that disturb and modify them, in many cases negatively.

PART 1 –
THEORETICAL
AND STATISTICAL
REFLECTIONS ABOUT THE
IMMIGRATION PROCESS
AND ITS PSYCHOLOGICAL
IMPLICATIONS

1

REFLECTIONS ABOUT THE HISTORY OF IMMIGRATION IN THE UNITED STATES AND THE WORLD

According to the dictionary, migration consists of the act of moving from one place to another, within the country or across borders, for people, birds, or insects. Immigration describes the act of an individual or family moving to a new country from their country of origin due to formalities at the embassy. Therefore, the difference between migration and immigration is solely due to economical and political facets of our modern world, but they are the same phenomena in essence and psychological implications.

So, in fact, the history of human immigration started around 2,000,000 years ago, with the exit of *Homo erectus* from Africa, followed by the Heidelbergensis, likely the ancestors of modern humans and Neanderthals. Finally, *Homo sapiens* ventured from Africa toward Europe around 250,000 years ago, spreading also around Asia 75,000 years ago, and finally arriving in the new continents and islands since then. Other studies show that the Heidelbergensis left Africa and the group subdivided soon after. A group followed northwest toward Asia and Europe, originating the Neanderthals, and another group went east, becoming the Denisovans. Around 130,000 years ago, the Heidelbergensis in Africa became *Homo sapiens*. According to those studies, modern man did not initiate his exit from Africa until 60,000 years ago, when they spread around Eurasia, meeting their cousins there. Some scientists suggest that modern man adapted better, or exterminated his Neanderthal cousin through competition. But new genetic evidence suggests that they simply procreated with each other, originating new generations with physical traits predominantly similar to modern man. In a study from 2011 from Stanford University, researchers concluded that many of us carry Neanderthal genes and that the majority of Europeans carry from 1% to 11% of Neanderthal DNA. Only indigenous Africans from the sub-Sahara carry no Neanderthal DNA, as their ancestors did not migrate to Eurasia.

Besides the numerous changes in perspective and understanding of humanity from the point of view of the archeological, bio-genetic, and historical evolution, those new scientific data bring to the surface some obvious facts, distorted and ignored by modern history, due to political, ideological, and economic agendas. Those indisputable facts are:

1) All of us, without exception, have African genes, since our species originated in Africa.
2) There is no such thing as an Aryan or pure Caucasian race. To the contrary, archeology, genetics, and history prove us, without a doubt, that individuals with a light complexion (skin and hair), were originated much later in the history of humankind from genetic mutations, and therefore they are the ones who carry the most diverse types of DNA in their genes, but not the most evolved characteristics.
3) Such racial characteristics (of Caucasians or Aryans) presenting their bio-types through recessive genes, which, evolutionarily speaking, are not the most favorable for the adjustment and evolution of our species. That is due to the fact that those characteristics do not optimize the survival of individuals through all kinds of environmental conditions, and therefore do not promote the survival of our species.
4) Therefore, based on natural reasons alone, the Caucasian or Aryan race is more prone to extinction much sooner than all the other races.

Continuing on our analysis of the historical and archeological process of our planet, we see that the composition and position of the continents have undergone tremendous transformation since the pre-historical eras. Asia and Europe formed a great massive land (Eurasia). The glacial eras triggered the emergence of huge volumes of land, which connected Eastern Asia to what we know now as the Americas, enabling the movement by land of *Homo sapiens*, who were able to populate all the major continents. There is archeological evidence that paleo-indigenous people arrived in North America, coming from Siberia, around fifteen thousand years ago, through nomadic explorations, spreading afterward down through Central and South America.

The neuro-bio-anatomical evolution of primates led them to create and to refine their hunting and self-defense instruments and utensils, and led also to the discovery of fire. Such discoveries and conquests created the conditions to initiate and progressively succeed in the migratory movements.

The scientist Christopher Henshilwood from Bergen University in Norway affirmed that "such movements of exploration of new lands represented a determinant factor for the human dominant status over nature, giving the human species the ability to perpetuate themselves and to dominate the other species, and giving them enormous advantages in the adaptation process on our planet." Immigration, therefore, is a recurrent, adaptive, and natural phenomenon of improvement of the human race, searching for survival and diversity. Such movement brought us even more significant benefits throughout the whole process, by providing us with diversity within our species, which grants us great adaptative advantages, resistance, and longevity of the species as a whole.

Throughout history, evolutionary quests led the human species to the development of verbal language, discovery of new natural instruments, the refinement of artifacts, the development of social organizations, and a wider comprehension of the world until the advent of sciences, systems, and methods of production and more complex social and political organizations.

The explorations of new territories in search of survival or expansion of power and dominance, allied to the multiplication of the human population in the already populated territories, generated different movements of exploration and population, which succeeded one another. The cognitive evolutionary development of humanity transformed the nature of territorial expansions and explorations of natural resources, which started to be determined not only by survival reasons but motivated by reasons of power and socio-political dominance.

Eras later, new socio-political-economic needs and realities determined new migratory movements, such as the expansion of the Babylonian, Egyptian, and Roman empires; the rise of Christianity, forcing thousands of new Christians to cross new frontiers due to religious-political persecutions, the Spanish and Portuguese crusades to the Americas looking for economic exploitation of the natural wealth of Central and South Americas, and the invasion of North America by the British in search for religious freedom. Once more here we can notice new partners of immigration.

Through this panoramic observation of the history of humankind we can easily see that in reality, immigration is the norm and not the exception of human behavior, since prehistoric times to the present. Not only is it the norm, but a necessity to guarantee our continuous diversity and adaptability on the planet. Beyond the evolution acquired through the geno-biological changes to adjust to different environments, medicine and genetics also show that cross-racial matings promote new, better-adjusted, and stronger genomes, assuring again the survival of the human species. It is scientifically observed in cases of intra-racial mating, in enclosed groups, for religious, cultural or ideological reasons. Like among the Orthodox Jews, royal families, the Amish, etc., where consanguinity and inbreeding starts to happen, and with it a significant increase of genetic diseases, infertility, and even, the deterioration of the phenotypes starts to happen within a few generations, growing exponentially from generation to generation. The opposite can also be observed, when children of bi-racial parents are statistically healthier and more beautiful.

Let us focus now on the migratory movements of

North America. It is registered that the Vikings settled in what is now called North America around the year 1000 A.D. In the mid-15th century, the Spanish Christopher Colombus discovered the Caribbean Islands and Central America, and at the end of the 15th century an Italian commissioned and sponsored by the Spanish crown, Amerigo Vespucci, "discovered" the Americas. According to historical data, many of Vespucci's letters that were spread through Europe, which a German cartographer used as a basis to create the first map of South America in 1507, were found to be a fraud.

In 1607 the first British colony was founded in Jamestown, Virginia. England at that time was passing through reforms, resistance, and political-religious separatist movements, which brought instability to the European scene. Many Puritans who disagreed with the mandatory homogeneity and officialization of the Anglican church in England had run to the Netherlands to pursue religious freedom. However, their need to maintain their cultural British roots brought them to reach for sponsors and partners with British investors to form colonies in the North America, in order to preserve both their religious freedom and their cultural integrity. With this intent, in 1620, the first pilgrims settled in Plymouth, Massachusetts. The small *Mayflower* ship came ashore at Plymouth Bay in autumn of that year, with 120 passengers on board, including men, women, and children. They brought some food, household and personal supplies. During the first winter, a few months later, half of that population died of hunger, thirst, and disease. The food supplies they brought with them deteriorated, they did not have access to water other than the sea, and the harsh freezing winter did not allow them to explore the natural resources of the area and harvest for their maintenance during the winter.

Their wooden hovels, straw roofs, and dirt floors offered them little comfort or protection against the weather. The colony, as expected, had a small chapel as the central building, where they gathered to keep their religious practices and freedom, as they wished. The modest chapel, however, supported at its second floor a fort with cannons to protect them from "invaders" (according to the books), the indigenous people, seen and treated as rivals and competitors for the limited resources of the region. The Dutch, French, and other European invasions were insignificant compared to the attacks toward the Natives, who were, in fact, the ones who suffered the invasion of their lands.

After centuries of massacres of the indigenous people, and approximately ten years of war against the British, the Declaration of Independence of the United States was proclaimed and the dissident British Pilgrims, who started to identify themselves as Americans, took official possession of part of the North American territory.

Its important here to highlight the precepts and means by which the country was founded: through force, in unfair competition with the Natives and in violent conflicts between the two factions of British (pro and against the British crown). The USA carries an intrinsic vocation for war in its British roots, and this is reflected throughout its history, in ceaseless internal and external tensions, persecutions, attacks, and rivalries.

Mass immigrations, especially from groups from the south and east of Europe, have succeeded since then. The avalanches of Europeans who arrived in the USA at the beginning of the 20th century raised concerns from the American authorities, and on 1917 the Immigration Act was decreed, through which it became a mandatory requirement for immigrants to be literate in their own language and be submitted to a rigorous medical examination, before going on board at the European ports toward America. With the two World Wars, numerous European immigrants reached shelter at the new continent (the Americas), including the USA. After World War II, large contingents of European immigrants, especially from Ireland and Italy, started again to invade the New York haven, running away from the devastating economic misery, hunger, and poverty prevailing in those countries at that time. They were mostly from the lower working classes with no professional qualifications. They got settled in degrading urban centers and assumed minimally paid positions. Among families and single men, there were also European women (mainly Dutch, Italian, German and Irish) who searched for a chance of survival in America after having their families exterminated in the war.

As if all the losses in Europe were not enough, in America, the ones who were allowed to stay suffered great discrimination, and often became victims of slavery, being obliged to work at whorehouses in exchange for food and shelter, as their owners were the only ones who would pay the port authorities to allow them to stay instead of being deported. The deportation would represent their own life sentences, as their survival at the war and during the long ship travel, in unsanitary and sickening conditions were already an immense stroke of luck. All this because they were there unaccompanied by a male figure- a father, a brother or a husband; regardless of the reasons why they ended up that way, not being with a man would automatically qualify them as women of questionable reputation.

After World War II, the Italians and Irish, the larger minorities of that time, were discriminated against, marginalized, and not wanted at all in America. They were the illegal immigrants of the mid-20th century, seen as the disease of American society, third-class "citizens", representing a threat to the national order and stability. It was very common for first generation Italian immigrants to deprive their children of speaking and learning their parents' native language and denying their ethnic origins in their daily lives, forcefully making their family fit into the local culture, due to the discrimination they suffered.

As Europe started to recover economically from the devastation of the wars, the European immigration waves started to fade, although they still continued to happen, as many of those countries never fully recovered after that and still have not recovered to this day, especially the countries considered the poor European nations, such as Italy, Portugal, Holand, Poland, Ireland and others that still suffer with unemployment, lack of infrastructure, inflation and lack of economic opportunities.

The rise of the USA as a world economic power had an opposite trajectory. The liberal government, the greed and individualistic attitude of a minority of visionaries, gave birth to illusory national power and wealth, as in fact the profits of this exponential growth were and continue to be centralized in the hands of financial oligarchies.

Cornelius Vanderbilt, whose great-grandparents immigrated to America in 1650, leaving the rural poverty of the Netherlands, accumulated his fortune through the construction of New York Central Station, opened in 1871, which was expanded to other states, promoting the development of those areas. John Rockefeller, son of German immigrants, opened an oil refinery in Cleveland, Ohio in 1863, expanding it throughout the country through the implantation of the "Standard Refinery", which created a monopoly on oil provided to heat American homes. Henry Ford, son of Irish and grandson of British immigrants, revolutionized the automobile industry through mass production in America. The list could go on--however we can point out the essential characteristics that all of those personalities who built the American economy and power consistently pursued:

1) Although obvious, many make sure to ignore the fact that all of them were descended from immigrants, who came to America searching for survival and a better life.

2) Regardless of a few philanthropic gestures, they all pursued a fierce greed in their character, and an aggressively competitive spirit, insatiable for wealth and power, dealing with all who were rising in prosperity, with brutal violent measures to destroy them, planning and executing Machiavellian strategies among themselves, as each one of them alone want to gain and control all the wealth and power, in absolute, sociopathic, individualistic manner. Growing and progressing were not enough. The destruction of ALL other successful personalities was their main goal in life.

3) In ironic development of the original motives that brought the first Pilgrims to America, the religious rigid morals soon disappeared from American culture, economy, and politics, being converted into ferocious greed, individualism, love and worship for wealth and power, and hatred toward their neighbors. It fits much better into the freedom of the diabolic fantasies

of those repressed groups who started ruling their conduct, aspirations and ethics through the most nobleless, anti-christian and holyless moral codes.

4) Due to the intransigent and ruthlessly destructive characteristics of the personalities who built America, political power soon became centralized in the hands of economic oligarchies, which determine the laws, manipulating the legislative, judiciary, and executive powers of the country to this day.

From the end of the 20th century until now, most of the migratory waves toward the USA have been from Latin America. With the economic crisis triggered by the war after the 9/11 terrorist attack in 2002, immigration restrictions in the USA were significantly intensified. On the other hand, the devastation of Mexico and all the Central and South American economies, caused by the globalization of the world's economy, continue to create intense need for those people to immigrate to the USA. The small and medium producers and businesses from every sector of the economy do not stand a chance of survival against the international oligarchies that more and more are becoming international monopolies. Those contrary forces generated a higher incidence of illegal immigrants in America, as their need for survival outpaces to their inability to acquire legal ways of doing it, where they can find it – outside of their countries.

Currently, as were the Irish and the Italians in the mid-20th century, the immigrants from Latin America, legal or illegal, are the ones considered third-class citizens of America. Ironically, most third- and fourth-generation immigrant descendants from Europe nowadays ignore their immigrant origins, with Italians being the most prejudiced against the new immigrants, seemingly oblivious to the fact that their ancestors, only a few decades ago, arrived in the USA in the same or worse conditions, clutching at survival and running from poverty.

The current scenario of immigration distribution in America is as follows, according to the US Census Bureau:

Figure 1. US Foreign-Born Population Overall and Unauthorized, by Country/Region of Origin, (%), 2009-13

ALL IMMIGRANTS	UNAUTHORIZED IMMIGRANTS
Mexico - 29%	Mexico - 56%
Asia – 29%	Asia – 14%
Europe/Canada/Oceania – 14%	Europe/Canada/Oceania - 4%
Caribbean - 9%	Caribbean – 2%
Central America - 8%	Central America – 15%
South America - 7%	South America – 6%
Africa - 4%	Africa – 3%

2

IMMIGRATION AND GLOBALIZATION

Immigration and territorial disputes are generators of conflict in humanity, as they are among animals, since the beginning of time. Through history, those disputes have become more and more complex, due to cultural, economic, social and political changes.

Our present world is characterized by drastic and fast changes at all levels. Technological developments, including communication, promote the complex phenomenon of globalization, much mentioned but little understood in its full extension and repercussions. Far from being a group of isolated facts reflecting the external market, which concerns only economists, corporations, and politicians, it affects the lives of all and each one of us as well as the destiny of our planet. We will focus here only on the aspects related to immigration.

By analyzing the reality of globalization and its

impact on the world's economy, we observe that the more this economic-political reality is disseminated, the more international boundaries between countries are controlled by corporations, which strengthen themselves and grow by leaps into entities of immeasurable power. Counting economic and political incentives from diverse countries with which they partner, as well as access to cheap supplies and labor, they make their profits and political-economic powers unstoppable, devouring local business and progressively annihilating it from the world economic scene.

Overtaken in frenetic saga of production increase and efficiency, in order to meet the passionate demands of the world market, along with the low cost of supplies and production, and the utilization of top technologies, including robotics, these factors all cause a shortage of jobs at all levels of the economy, and bring a significant decrease in the cost of the final products, making it impossible for local business to compete, and damaging the world economy as a whole.

On this wheel of fortune, the survival of everyday people, especially from the working classes, is compromised. In the USA alone this discrepancy explosively grew in the last decade. The concentration of wealth in the hands of the corporate class, which represents only 1% of the total American population, is equivalent to all the wealth of 50% of the total population combined, thanks to tax cuts for the corporations, which accumulate more and more wealth, without creating any beneficial return to the overall population and social system. On the other hand, the middle and lower classes of the population suffer with heavier and heavier tax burdens, and face increased cost of living, along with frozen salaries for years. In these ways, their purchasing power and standard of living have been cruelly smashed year after year.

The percentage of the world's population within the low-income class, living in poverty and misery, grows, while the concentration of wealth in the hands of the economic corporate oligarchies increases in geometric proportions. The so-called third-world countries, are the most affected and victimized in this process.

At the same proportion that international boundaries disappear for corporations, those same frontiers get stronger and more rigid for the rest of the population. In other words, globalization is a phenomenon acceptable to the powerful and wealthy, but not for the poor or average citizen. The immigrant is seen and rejected, even by the general population, as a threat to the local order and economy, as if they are stealing places in the local job market and public resources. However, the real destruction of the local orders, economy and stability, as well as the causers of the immigration and the economic crisis of our present time are due to the destructive and predatory rules of globalization by the corporations and its devastating effects on the local job markets and local economies in general, inside and outside of the USA.

The immigrant, for the most part, does not wish to leave their local land. The vast majority of them would not subject themselves to the risk, pain, loss, difficulty, and uncertainty of crossing foreign borders, if they had a choice to stay and have their and their family's basic needs met.

One example of that is the massive immigration of Mexicans to the USA. In the last decades, the competition between local farmers with American produce, livestock producers and industrialized merchandise, manufactured by multi-national industries, have made local production impractical. Therefore, they have no alternative but to immigrate to the USA to look for means of survival for themselves and their families. Statistics show that the number of Mexican immigrants in the USA increased from 760,000 to 12.7 million from 1970 to 2008.

In documentary made with the community of Michoaca in Mexico, it was verified that half of their population works in the USA. Most of them are from rural regions. The economy of those regions used to be based on the production of strawberries, wheat, corn, beans, soy, and swine. Currently, due to competition with American mass producers, which make their products much more affordable than those from local farmers, they broke, having to abandon their farms, and immigrated to the USA to survive and to support their families. They went bankrupt and due to their lack of education, or qualification in other professional fields, along with the shortage of jobs in surrounding cities for the same reasons, they had no other means of survival.

The 2009 statistics on Brazilian immigration data, from the Itamaraty and the Brazilian Federal Ministry of International Relations, reported that there are around 3 million Brazilians living in other countries. The USA leads with the highest concentration of Brazilian immigrants, followed by Paraguay (with 300 thousand) and Japan (with 280 thousand). The Brazilians alone contributed this year with around US $55 billion of the USA Gross National Product.

From the 2010 Brazilian census (IBGE official data), the numbers dropped to 2.5 billion Brazilians living outside of Brazil. The USA has 23.8%, Portugal 13.4%, Spain 9.4%, Japan 7.4%, Italy 7.0% and England 6.2%. Of the total, 53.8% are women and 46.1% are men. Considering the Brazilian immigrants spread through the world, the statistics by regional origins are: 1st place from the southeast with 49% of the total, being 21.6% from São Paulo, 16.8% from Minas Gerais and 7.1% from Rio de Janeiro. 2nd place from the south with 17,2%, followed by the northeast with 15%, center west with 12%, and the north with 6.9% of the total. In the USA, the majority of Brazilian immigrants come from Minas Gerais state (43.2%), followed by Rio de Janeiro (30.6%), Goiás (22.6%), São Paulo (20.1%) and Paraná (16.6%).

3

THE IMMIGRANT AND COMMUNICATION

Communication is, without a doubt, one of the most important factors of the social adaptation and integration of human reality in general, ever since the early days of civilization. Communication requires the utilization of language. Linguistic science, which studies language, brings different definitions of the concept of language.

The view of the structuralist Fernand de Saussure describes language as a formal system of signs, guided by grammatical rules which, when combined, generate meanings. This definition understands the language as a closed structural system, constituted of rules that relate specific signs with specific meanings (Roy, 1989). In other words, this is the concept of language most similar to the common sense: a group of written and phonetic information, easily acquired through the memorization of signs, phonemes, and grammatical rules. This definition reduces the learning of a language to learning the words, symbols, pronunciation, and their utilization to express thoughts between individuals, completely ignoring the cultural, circumstantial, interpersonal and non-verbal contexts, and aspects of human communication. For the most part, that is the basis of the training to prepare professional travelers, such as the executives of international corporations, or even individuals preparing themselves to move to another country. Although acquisition of language is an indisputably important factor toward the adjustment into another culture, we will see at the end of this chapter that communication goes far beyond proficiency with a language.

Its not uncommon for us to hear stories of individuals who develop foreign language skills for years, became fluent in every level, but facing practical situations, such as visiting or moving to another country that utilizes that language, go through a process of regression in their verbal performance. Common sense understand this phenomenon as due to the different accents of each country and region or the dialects and peculiarities of the colloquial language. However, a more detailed analysis of those events shows us that it entails something much more complex and deeper, which goes beyond cognition or a simple momentary shyness or nervousness, which we will discuss a little later in this chapter.

The cognitive and interactive linguistic approach, the sociolinguistic and the anthropologic linguistic, describe the language as a communication system that allows human beings to share their senses. This view highlights the social function of language and the fact that human beings utilize it to express themselves to one another and to relate with their social environment. It considers the social context and the interpersonal interactions as integrating aspects of the communication, turning it, therefore, into a dynamic and interactive phenomenon, instead of a mere structure of symbols and rules, immune and static to the nuances coming from the communicator and the recipient during the communication process.

Since World War I, contemporary psychology has demonstrated a considerable interest in the communication phenomenon. The Freudian school of psychology tends to associate communication interactions as a reverberation of the family dynamic group, experienced during childhood. The behaviorists are going toward an understanding of communication in terms of stimuli-response between the sources of communication and the recipient individuals or groups.

In the mid-1950s, psychology started to concentrate great interest in the persuasive aspects of communication. Some approaches developed studies of the recipient of communication, involving concepts of selective perception and selective retention to explain not only the forms in which communication changes attitudes, but also the reasons that cause resistance to change.

The social psychologist Leon Festinger developed the concept of "cognitive dissonance", through the observation of individuals from diverse socio-ethnic origins. The presentation of recurrent intolerance, above a certain degree of discrepancy in the perception of their environment, was evident. Those schools turned their attention to the comprehension of communication phenomena in light of reality distortions by subjective factors of the recipient and of the communicator and, as a consequence, the observation of the distortion of perception of the received messages. Such subjective factors arise unconsciously, with the purpose of attending the individual's needs, to align external with internal realities and to accomodate one's external reality to one's understanding of self and the world, all pre-established through one's history and genetics. Consider an example of cognitive dissonance: A person who considers himself very self-confident about his skill as a basketball player faces a bad performance during a game. He tries to modify his perception of the reality, utilizing weather factors, the conditions of the court, or defects of the ball to try to explain and to justify his poor performance, with the objective to decrease the inner tension caused by such dissonance.

The social, body psychology, the psychodrama, Gestalt, and other psychological theories, approach communication in a even wider way. Regardless of the different concepts and precepts of each, they all have in common a consideration of the subjectivity, emotions, social context, as well as cultural, historical, circumstantial, and physiological aspects of individuals and groups.

As an example, we can return to the situation mentioned above, in which the individual loses temporarily his/her capacity for a good verbal performance when visiting or migrating to a country that utilizes a foreign language in which he/she was proficient. The quantity and intensity of new stimuli to which this individual is exposed, captured unconsciously by his senses, consume an unimaginable percentage of his physiological and mental functions. The sum of all those sensory-psychological-social stimuli, such as new smells, atmospheric pressure, temperatures, and visual, auditorial, kinetic, vibrational, and tactile stimuli, unconsciously absorb the individual's attention and energy, in order to process everything, and this compromises what he/she expected to deliver verbally and cognitively.

To better illustrate that there is a vast quantity of subliminal stimuli received from the environment, which are assimilated unconsciously into our ways of function at the physical, emotional and energetic levels, we can mention an experiment made with North American and European college students by a prominent Canadian music professor, in order to verify the effects of geographic location on sound perception and production. The students were instructed, in individual encounters, to vocalize the first musical note that came to their minds. The North Americans all produced B flat and all the Europeans G sharp. The professor then observed that in the USA, electric voltage is 60 cycles per second, which corresponds very closely to the frequency of a very low B flat, while the electrical voltage in Europe is 50 cycles per second, which is very close to G sharp. This brings to our awareness the infinite number of factors, perceived unconciously by our senses from the environment in each geographic location, which have a great impact and influence on one's psychological and physiological functionality (Pearce, 2008).

Note Frequencies

Table of frequencies in Hz of the musical pitches. The numbers in the left are the octaves. It uses an even tempered scale with A=440 Hz.

	C	C#	D	Eb	E	F	F#	G	G#	A	Bb	B
0	16.35	17.32	18.35	19.45	20.60	21.83	23.12	24.50	25.96	27.50	29.14	30.87
1	32.70	34.05	36.71	38.89	41.20	43.65	46.25	49.00	51.91	55.00	58.27	61.74

We receive, absorb, and internalize numerous influences from our social and physical environment, which become part of our metabolism in visceral ways through the years. When we face environmental changes, besides the conscious physical and mental adjustments, we are also bombarded by numerous new stimuli, captured only at visceral and unconscious levels, but which nevertheless consume a large quantity of energy to be processed.

Psychology also brings to the surface the physical or corporeal aspect of communication, ignored by linguistics. Corporeal language is a very important aspect in communication process for a majority of the species, including humans. Gestures, body and facial expressions, distance and proximity, as well as physical and eye contact are crucial aspects of human communication. We observe through the development of cultural psychology that their meanings significantly differ, and can even be opposite from one culture to another. (Collett, 1982; Morris, 1979) For example, in the USA and practically all the American continent, signing giving a thumbs up corresponds to an approval sign. In Greece, the same gesture means a great insult, associated to the expression "*katsa pano*" or "sit on this." Another example is the sign made by bringing the tip of the thumb with the tip of second finger together, making a circle. In the USA it means OK or approval. In Brazil, is an obscene gesture corresponding to "screw yourself."

Most of the Latino--especially Brazilian--immigrants' difficulties and frustrations, in regard to communication in America is related to body language and voice placement. North Americans usually present flat facial expressions, and are very reserved about physical contact, even with their close and intimate ones. Americans communicate with throat vocal placement, with very minimal expression of emotions, and a flat facial and body expressions. Brazilians, on the other hand, present chest and frontal vocal placement, easily express emotions, and physical touches are constant and an integrated part of communication, even in professional or formal contexts. In general, the corporeal aspects and the vocal placements are not even mentioned in processes of learning a foreign language. However, by becoming aware of those facts, it is easy for anyone to imagine the great discomfort and lapses of communication due to those non-verbal messages.

Latinos and Brazilians, with their warm attitudes and behavior, are wrongly seen, heard, and perceived as cognitively inferior, as the spontaneous physical contact intrinsic to their ways of communicating is translated by Caucasian Americans as inappropriate or sexually driven. Latinos and Brazilians, on another hand, oblivious to such judgements and misperceptions, feel isolated and find comfort associating with other immigrants who share similar values and codes of communication. Caucasians are perceived by Latinos and Brazilians, as cold, flat, distant and emotionless. If a close and fulfilling social network with similar cultures is not possible for some reason, the lack of physical contact and expression of emotional connection in their social relationships with Caucasians causes a sensation of emptiness, social isolation, or even depression.

The Anglo-Saxon culture, especially the Puritans,

who are the roots of the culture in the Northeast of the USA, left very rigid limits when it comes to expression of emotion, the use of the body, and physical contact in public. Learning about the costumes and beliefs of the first immigrants from England to the USA was very useful to my adjustment process in the Northeast. The Puritans, as we mentioned before, tried to impose their religious values on the Anglican church during King Henry VIII's government. Through the "Supremacy Act" and being severely persecuted, they came to the USA in search of religious freedom. The Puritans' religious values included absolute separation from the liturgy and traditions of the Catholic church, the spiritual equality of husband and wife before God, and total abstinence from any expression of affect and emotion, as a reflection of a life of penitence and spirituality. Music and utilization of musical instruments were banned from their religious rituals. Expressions of affect such as an smile, a hug, holding hands, or any other form of facial expression, physical contact, or expression of emotions, even among family members, were considered sinful and subject to public punishment.

Such practices, values, and conditioned learned behaviors, severely imposed into the New England cultural roots, clearly persists in Anglo-Saxon American behavior to this day. When we relate to individuals emotionally warmer, spontaneous, and expressive, most likely they have a Latino, Italian, Portuguese, Spanish, Irish, or Scottich background.

The Latinos and Brazilians, with Spanish and Portuguese roots, and also with some French and Italian influences, carry opposite values. They are much more flexible, with behavioral and relationship norms much expressive and warm. Its considered rude and anti-social not to reply to a received smile, hug, or kiss on the cheek in formal or informal social encounters, both between friends or strangers. Keeping and inert body, flat facial expression, low tone and monotone voice while communicating with others, which are the norm in the Northeast of the USA, in Latin America is considered inappropriate and an absence of interpersonal skills, similar to individuals with personality or neurological disorders.

Brazil especially, with tropical weather and its natural richness and beauty, only compared to its vast continental proportions, attracted and still attracts individuals interested in enjoying a pleasant and upbeat lifestyle. The first settlers, upon arrival at what was then called Vera Cruz Island, encountered naked, peaceful, friendly, and festive indigenous people. The massive devastation of the natives are as much due to genocide in disputes for territory from the Europeans as to the vocation for peace of the indigenous people, along with the many diseases brought by the Europeans, to which the native people had not built immunological defenses.

Stories and letters about the first group of ships led by Pedro Alvares Cabral anchoring in Brazil, describe the indigenous people coming close to the colonists, exploring those strange, bad-smelling, white-skinned visitors, dressed in weird attire. After entering in the ship, many of them simply made themselves comfortable and fell asleep aboard the ship. Such was the spirit of community and cooperation to which they were accustomed among themselves.

Besides the exploitation of the natural resources of the land, the Portuguese royalty and elite found themselves settling at their tropical retreat in Brazil. Royalty migrated in large groups, developing the northern region as an extension of Portugal where they could live. They built cities like Manaus in the Amazon and Belem in Pará, with refined architecture desirable to the Portuguese elite, with a large and luxurious Opera House, commercial centers, and all the sophistication offered in Europe during the 15th and 16th centuries. Comfort and sophistication, along with the advantages of a natural paradise, were able to provide them with an abundant and easy life, with plenty of natural resources and freedom. The new country gained prominent desirability among them.

Although almost exterminated, the friendly and pacific predisposition of the indigenous people, impregnated the cultural roots of the "Santa Cruz land", along with desirable European aspirations of an easy and abundant life full of pleasure, combined over the centuries to create what today we know as the Brazilian people. Those historical trajectories can trace behavioral, interpersonal, and social codes, that value friendliness, pleasure, prosperity, and happiness.

In contrast, the British colonization of the USA has its foundation in war, persecution, and disputes, before and after their arrival in the new land. The bitter and harsh weather offered few natural resources and little comfort, and the need for them to create a livable infrastructure, with great suffering, led them to develop an introspective, reserved, and conservative attitude. Virgin lands, with harsh weather and deprived from natural resources, would not attract exploitation colonialists. Those went to Central and South America. The settlers in North America just looked for freedom from the British crown to build their own set of rules, laws, and religion.

The Pilgrims, then, besides of facing adversities of conquering the new land, diseases to which they had no immunity, and lack of resources and sponsorship, started to be deeply exploited by the British government, after being defeated by Spain and Portugal in its numerous attempts to invade Central and South America. The British crown adopted the new colony in North America as their only chance to exploit and take advantage of the New World. The heavy and escalating taxes charged by the British government to the new settlers, brutally enforced by the crown's army, became more and more oppressing to them. There were battles as they tried to free themselves from this oppression and exploitation. Along with the already difficult circumstances they were facing, adjusting to the New World, this whole reality forced them to detach themselves even more from their own emotions, as a self-preservation defense mechanism.

Imagine now those two realities meeting four or five centuries later. The exponential differences of language, perception of self and the world, emotional and psychological backgrounds, and subjective distances of those realities and cultures, create an abysmal gap between those two groups, preventing them from truly understanding and relating to each other closely. All those aspects have a very important role in communication process.

Both sides, Latinos and Anglo-Saxon Americans, proceed without taking into consideration their origin, cultural contexts, as well as historical and collective baggage. They also ignore the fact that the harmonious blending of both cultures would result in enormous advantages for everyone in a journey toward success and happiness.

Only through the development of such perceptive refinement can we in fact develop a common language, not only hearing but being able to listen and fully understand and learn with each other--to be able to understand that we all have been through similar processes of immigration in search of a better life, one way or another, and we all present similar needs and aspirations of happiness, abundance, prosperity, without fear or suffering, reaching peace and sustainability.

4

THE IMMIGRANT
AND LABOR

According to official data from the 2013 American census, the foreign worker (born outside of USA) makes in average 79.9% less then the Caucasian born in America, to perform the same job. (Bureau of Labor Statistics) In this average, men and women, immigrants from every part of the world, legal or illegal, are included. When we isolate the Latino population and further split out the ones with work visas or citizenship, the differences increase exponentially.

USA

CHARACTERISTICS	2008	2009	2010	2011	2012
Foreign born					
Total, 16 years and over	68.1	67.9	67.9	67.0	66.3
Men	81.4	80.5	80.1	79.5	78.5
Women	54.8	55.4	55.7	54.6	54.8
RACE					
Black non-Hispanic or Latino	60.3	59.8	60.7	60.2	60.1
White non-Hispanic or Latino	73.2	72.4	74.6	71.2	70.6
Hispanic or Latino	70.7	70.8	70.8	69.8	69.0

EDUCATIONAL LEVEL (age 25 years and over)

	2008	2009	2010	2011	2012
Less than high school diploma	61.1	61.4	61.6	60.0	59.9
High school graduates, no college	68.1	67.2	68.4	66.8	66.4
Some college or associate degree	73.7	73.7	73.4	72.9	71.0
Bachelor's degree and higher	77.0	76.9	75.5	75.7	75.3

CHARACTERISTICS	2008	2009	2010	2011	2012
NATIVE BORN					
Total, 16 and over	65.6	64.9	64.1	63.6	63.2
Men	71.4	70.4	69.5	68.8	68.6
Women	60.3	59.8	59.1	58.7	58.2
RACE					
White non-Hispanic or Latino	66.2	65.7	64.8	64.3	63.7
Black non-Hispanic or Latino	62.5	61.2	60.7	60.1	60.0

Asian non-Hispanic or Latino	62.7	61.0	61.5	61.5	61.5
Hispanic or Latino	66.1	65.0	64.0	63.2	63.9

EDUCATIONAL LEVEL (Age 25 years and over)

Less than a high school diploma	38.4	37.9	37.1	37.7	36.7
High school graduates, no college	61.8	61.4	60.6	59.3	58.4

INTERNATIONAL COMPARISSON

USA

Indicator	Unit	2010	2011	2012
Costs in manufacturing				
Hourly compensation	US dollars	34.81	35.51	35.67
Hourly pay for time worked	US dollars	23.31	23.69	23.93
Hourly compensation costs	US dollars	34.81	35.51	35.67
Hourly directly paid benefits	US dollars	3.86	4.05	4.11
Hourly Social Security expenditures and labor-related taxes	US dollars	4.32	4.73	4.86

GERMANY

Indicator	Unit	2010	2011	2012
Costs in manufacturing				
Hourly compensation	US dollars	43.84	47.42	45.79
Hourly pay for time worked	US dollars	25.80	27.70	26.45
Hourly directly paid benefits	US dollars	8.45	9.48	9.62
Hourly Social Security expenditures and labor-related taxes	US dollars	9.59	10.24	9.73

FRANCE

Indicator	Unit	2010	2011	2012
Costs in manufacturing				
Hourly compensation	US dollars	39.12	42.12	39.81
Hourly pay for time worked	US dollars	20.16	21.70	20.51
Hourly directly paid benefits	US dollars	7.25	7.80	7.38
Hourly Social Security expenditures and labor-related taxes	US dollars	11.71	12.61	11.92

PORTUGAL

Indicator	Unit	2010	2011	2012
Costs in manufacturing				
Hourly compensation	US dollars	11.94	13.15	12.10
Hourly pay for time worked	US dollars	7.29	8.03	7.39
Hourly directly paid benefits	US dollars	2.30	2.53	2.33
Hourly Social Security expenditures and labor-related taxes	US dollars	2.35	2.59	2.38

JAPAN

Indicator	Unit	2010	2011	2012
Costs in manufacturing				
Hourly compensation	US dollars	31.75	35.71	35.34
Hourly pay for time worked	US dollars	18.17	20.19	20.11
Hourly directly paid benefits	US dollars	7.84	9.06	8.83
Hourly Social Security expenditures and labor-related taxes	US dollars	5.75	6.46	6.40

BRAZIL

Indicator	Unit	2010	2011	2012
Costs in manufacturing				
Hourly compensation	US dollars	10.01	11.67	11.20
Hourly pay for time worked	US dollars	5.38	6.20	5.95
Hourly directly paid benefits	US dollars	1.43	1.64	1.58
Hourly Social Security expenditures and labor-related taxes	US dollars	3.20	3.83	3.67

ARGENTINA

Indicator	Unit	2010	2011	2012
Costs in manufacturing				
Hourly compensation	US dollars	12.77	15.98	18.87
Hourly pay for time worked	US dollars	8.76	10.96	12.94
Hourly directly paid benefits	US dollars	1.79	2.24	2.64
Hourly Social Security expenditures and labor-related taxes	US dollars	2.22	2.78	3.29

UNITED KINGDOM

Indicator	Unit	2010	2011	2012
Costs in manufacturing				
Hourly compensation	US dollars	29.11	30.77	31.23
Hourly pay for time worked	US dollars	20.93	21.98	22.27
Hourly directly paid benefits	US dollars	3.86	4.05	4.11
Hourly Social Security expenditures and labor-related taxes	US dollars	4.32	4.73	4.86

SUMARY OF HOURLY COMPENSATION COSTS IN MANUFACTURING

In 2012, according to the USA Bureau of Labor Statistics, this is the order of the main countries in regard to hourly compensation costs for manufacturing:

Norway	63.36	Spain	26.83
Switzerland	57.79	New Zealand	24.77
Belgium	52.19	Singapore	24.16
Sweden	49.80	Korea, Rep of.	20.72
Denmark	48.80	Israel	20.14
Australia	47.68	Greece	19.41
Germany	45.79	Argentina	18.87
Finland	42.60	Portugal	12.10
Austria	41.53	Czech Republic	11.95
France	39.81	Slovakia	11.30
Netherlands	39.62	Brazil	11.20
Ireland	38.17	Estonia	10.41
Canada	36.59	Taiwan	9.46
United States	35.67	Hungary	8.95
Japan	35.34	Poland	8.25
Italy	34.18	Mexico	6.36
United Kingdom	31.23	Philippines	2.10

The proportional work-related benefits of Brazilians (in Brazil) in comparison to Americans (in America) are significantly higher. Brazil is in 2nd place in the rank of the paid benefit international comparisons, with over 30% of social security expenditures and almost 15% of directly paid benefits. The Mexicans are in 4th place with 30% of government expenditures, but have almost no directly paid benefits. America is in 12th place with less than 25% of government expenditures and less then 10% of directly paid benefits. Therefore, contrary to what is commonly believed, the issue of financial hardship of those immigrants at their country of origin, prior to immigration is not related to the lack of socio-political infrastructure or lack of government efforts and regulations to protect their workers. It's most likely to be solely due to the devastating impact of the globalization on their economy.

China's manufacturing employment and hourly labor compensation, 2002-2009

In our current economic reality, China is the center pillar of global manufacturing. In 2006, China became the United States' second-largest trading partner in manufactured goods, after Canada. By 2010, it surpassed Japan, becoming the second-largest economy in the world.

In spite of the global economic crisis beginning in late 2008, China's manufacturing employment increased to 99 million in 2009. Though earnings for manufacturing enterprise employees in China were higher than in any previous year, average hourly compensation costs were only $1.74 in 2009. China's hourly compensation costs as of 2009 remained far bellow those of many of its East Asian neighbors such as Japan ($30.03), the Republic of Korea ($15.06), and Singapore ($17.54), but were roughly on par with those of the Philippines ($1.70). (Bureau of Labor Statistics)

INDIA

Compensation costs in India's organized manufacturing sector were 91 cents per hour for all employees in 2005; this amounted to about 3 % of hourly labor costs in the US manufacturing sector, but was above BLS estimates of labor costs in China. (Bureau of Labor Statistics)

The compensation for the immigrant labor, especially for undocumented workers, is low and paid hourly. Therefore, for them to accumulate a salary compatible with their goals of saving money to go back to their country of origin, to acquire a house, or to start their own business, they need to accumulate numerous hours of labor.

The male and female Brazilian immigrant in the USA works an average of 60 hours per week; it is very common among them to work 90 hours per week. They need to endure to less than ideal work conditions, with no benefits, guarantees, or worker's rights. Due to the long hours, and the physical stress associated with cultural, weather, and dietary adjustments, with no meal breaks, cases of accidents in the work place are numerous. Many jobs are in the manual labor fields, including construction and home renovations, landscaping, snow removal from sidewalks, driveways, yards, and roofs, as cook's assistants, servers, or dishwashers in restaurants, and as residential and commercial housekeepers. Workers in all of these fields are victims of accidents, which are sometimes fatal or disabling.

Besides the accumulated stress, which compromises their attention, concentration, and reflexes, it is common for them to be in the hands of employers who do not provide them with enough training or appropriate safety tools, required by law. Some of them take advantage of the vulnerability of the undocumented immigrants, not honoring their earned weekly pay and illegally firing them after an accident, without having their worker's rights honored, leaving them without any financial or medical assistance for treatment, counting on the fact that they will not be able to sue for fear of deportation.

The long work hours also leave little time for leisure, social or family activities. This deeply affects not only the worker's physical and mental health, but also their relationships and the physical and mental health of their family members, especially children. Their children are left after school in domestic day care, usually run by other immigrants, who, without proper training, lack the skill to provide the best care, emotional support, and intelectual stimuli for children to develop in healthy manner. When these children reach the age of twelve, they are left at home after school, without adult assistance or supervision, which sometimes generates emotional or behavioral problems in children and teenagers. This reality has caused an epidemic of cases of depression, anxiety, drug and alcohol abuse, and even suicide in adult and teenaged immigrants.

On the other hand, the ones who are able to run their own business in America gain success and financial independence, and in states like Massachusetts, the Brazilians have established a positive reputation in certain fields, such as construction, landscaping, and house cleaning, earning higher salaries than the local Americans.

According to official data from the 2014 American census, the average salary of the American family is $50,000/year, around $25,000/person.

25% of the families earn an anual income from 0 to $24,999

24% makes from $25,000 to $49,999/year,

18% makes from $50,000 to 74,999/year,

11.7% makes $75,000 to $99,999/year,

12.1% makes $100,000 to 149,000/year,

4.4% makes $150,000 to $200,000/year and

4.3% makes above $200,000/year.

More then 50% of the American population, therefore, live in a state of poverty, with frozen salaries for more than a decade, with 17% of the population depending on government assistance to buy food, while the concentration of wealth in the hands of the 10% richest grew exponentially in the last decade.

Even then, the financial growth of the Brazilian entrepreneur in America happens thanks to very long working hours, competitive prices of labor compared to the same services offered by most American companies, flexibility and techniques that enable them to optimize production, delivering better services in less time. Some of those small entrepreneurs come from a modest background and have low levels of education. Others carry a college degree, but need to be self-employed doing manual labor for lack of a green card or citizenship, which prevent them from getting a professional license in their field of training, or by option, as the manual labor fields are the ones that present better compensation in America.

The Brazilian house cleaners in America are able to execute a complete cleaning on three to five houses per day, thanks to techniques of optimization of their work, which they developed themselves or learned with one another. Usually the more experienced, self-labeled as "owners of the schedule," train the new ones, who sometimes have recently arrived from Brazil, and when those aquire proficiency, enough practice at the work, and better English, they build up their own "schedule" (their own companies), dealing directly with the homeowners or residents. The assistants are paid 1/5 to 1/10 of the price paid by the homeowner for the service.

In the construction field, the so-called Brazilian "handyman," in general learns and develops techniques by working initially as assistants in American or Brazilian companies, making very low initial salaries compared to the average in the market. Many of them gain proficiency in as many sectors of work as possible, including the legal codes of the American construction laws and regulations, in a short period of time. For example, when they are hired to perform painting services at a house, and they find moisture in the walls, they can verify if there is pipe leakage, fix it, and make sure the electric installation was not compromised; if so, they can fix it, and if the eventual leakage damaged the floors, they fix it, all before performing the final convenience to the client. Many of them are proficient in a wide array of construction sectors, painting, wall and insulation installation, floors (tile, carpet and hardwood), plumbing, electrical, roofing, ceiling, kitchen and bathroom renovation, doors, windows, cabinet installation, and building stairs and porches. The ones who pursue a green card or citizenship, with a good English proficiency, attend courses of specialization in one or more areas to gain their state licenses in that field. When they become an entrepreneur, they earn business, as they can deliver the best service, for lower prices than most American companies.

American workers or entrepreneurs, on the other hand, focus on one or two specializations and are not able to perform services in other sectors of construction.

That requires the client to hire multiple workers, which significantly increases the price of labor.

Those who come with careers and professional qualifications already established and well developed, carrying also a green card, citizenship, or work visa, generally adapt easily to the job market, which allows them to feel a lower impact of cultural shock, through their professional satisfaction and preservation of a big part of their identity. The compensation satisfaction of this population varies, depending on their level of professional experience, the overall culture and policies at their particular workplace, and the specific fields of work. The ones who complete their academic training in the USA and do not pursue previous professional experience in Brazil tend to report the most professional satisfaction in America. Those who came with previous professional experience in Brazil and moved to the USA for reasons other than their own choice (such as to accompany their partners or children) face lower levels of satisfaction and adjustment to life here. The weather, the distance from family and friends, the social isolation, and the much less active social lifestyle in America compared to the one experienced in Brazil, are the main factors that create dissatisfaction and adjustment difficulties to those Brazilian immigrants in the USA. Professional recognition and the achievement of a satisfactory social status through marriage or career development, financial status, as well as satisfaction in the marriage and family relationship, are essential compensatory factors to promote social and emotional adjustment for the immigrant.

5

THE IMMIGRANT AND EATING HABITS

For many, especially those who never experienced the acculturation process, the changes in eating habits due to translocation (geographic move), may seem of little importance, superficial and of no psychological implications. However, my experience working with immigrants, and my own experience, proved me the opposite. In Brazil, despite coming from a cosmopolitan city like São Paulo, having an intensive professional life, I was used to having five or six meals a day. During my last years there, before moving to the USA, this was my routine: I woke up around 6:00 a.m., got ready for work, and ate breakfast with fruit, milk, a slice of bread, or oatmeal, and left for the rehearsal of São Paulo Symphonic Choir, where I used to work as a professional singer. Around 10:00 a.m., we had a little break, when we all went to a coffee place close by and had a little snack with a cheese bread or a croquette and some juice. At the end of the practice, around 1:00 p.m., we had lunch with different vegetables, salad, some rice and beans, and some animal protein, all in small portions. Then I followed my day of work in my private psychology practice, where I saw clients until late at night. Around 3:30 p.m., I had another little break with some tea and a snack with fruit or yogurt, following my day until 7:00 or 9:00 p.m. The days we had concerts, I used to schedule fewer clients. On those days, I left the office around 4:00 or 5:00 p.m., stopped at home, a couple of minutes from the office, took a quick shower, changed clothes, had dinner, and went to the theater. After the concerts, sometimes I went out to a restaurant with my friends and co-workers or went back home and had a bedtime snack.

As soon as I arrived in the USA, my eating routine changed completely and I could feel the impact of it very shortly on my body. The changes were not only re-lated to the meal schedule (or lack of it!) but the quality of the meals as well. The American schedule is such that there is no real time for lunch or a snack. The dinner time is around 5:00 or 6:00 p.m. and up to that point the "lunches and snacks" are done as fast as possible, in transit, walking, driving, in public transportation or during a task (class or work). Nobody pays attention to what or how they are eating, and the meal times are not at all a pleasant or relaxed moment. Eating during the day is treated simply as an "inconvenient necessity" almost without importance in the list of priorities of the daily routine. Its considered a waste of time to seat on a table for a meal during business or school hours. Paradoxically, after those hours, eating becomes a consolation prize and immediate gratification for a hard, most of the time frustrating day of work. Then, the average American indulges themselves with the so called "comfort food," which is full of fat and/or sugar. Dinner time is generally in front of a TV or computer at home, and the eating process is not done at all in a mindful manner, which promotes overeating and poor absorption of nutrients.

Despite not having engaged completely in this mentality and these habits, the changes were inevitable, as there was no set time for the meals during the day. This, along with the stress of the daily routine, cost me some weight gain, less energy, and some digestive problems never experienced before, which affected my overall health for years until recently. Almost seventeen years later, I was able to regain a healthier lifestyle, thanks to some natural treatments which included food detox, changes of diet and being able to set my own schedule of meals. Back to my old schedule from Brazil, I lost a lot of weight and feel much more energized and healthier, physically and mentally.

According to numerous studies, stressful situations trigger the increase of appetite for some people. In general, they always cause significant metabolic changes, which trigger weight gain and generate diseases. The brain, as a way to compensate for mental stress, sends signals to increase food intake, to generate pleasure and decrease the levels of stress. (Marano, 2003, 2007)

In cases where the migratory process was a traumatic experience, the individual may develop eating disorders, such as anorexia (which along with self-deprivation of food, also involves a distortion of body image), bulimia, or obesity.

The treatment of such problems is very important and involves raising awareness and the resolution of emotional issues associated with them.

6

THE IMMIGRANT AND THE LAW

OFFICIAL DATA

Demographics (From US Census Bureau official data)

US Population (Jan 30. 2015):
320.244.755 (growing by the minute)

World Population (January 30, 2015):
7,221,022,300 (growing by the second)

Population, 2013 estimate MA= 6,692,824
USA= 316,128,839 persons.

Female Percent, 2013 Massachusetts= 51.5%
USA= 50.8%

Black or African-American alone, %, 2013 (a)
MA= 8.1% USA= 13.2%

Hispanic or Latino, %, 2013 MA= 10.5%
USA= 17.1%

Asian alone, %, 2013 MA= 6.0% USA= 5.3%

White alone, not Hispanic or Latino, %, 2013
MA= 75.1% USA= 62.6%

Foreign-born persons, %, 2009-2013 MA= 15.0%
USA= 12.9%.

In accordance with the USA National Highway Safety Administration, a traffic ticket is a notice issued by a law enforcement official to a motorist or other road user, accusing violation of traffic laws. Traffic tickets generally come in two forms, citing a moving violation, such as exceeding the speed limit, or a non-moving violation, such as a parking violation, with the ticket also being referred to as a parking citation, notice of illegal parking, or parking ticket.

The numbers reported by the USA NHSA in regard to driving citation statistics are:

Average number of people per day that receive a speeding ticket	112,000
Total annual number of people who receive speeding tickets	41,000,000

Total percentage of drivers that will get a speeding ticket this year	20.6%
Average cost of a speeding ticket (including fees)	$152
Total paid in speeding tickets per year	$6,232,000,000
Average annual speeding ticket revenue per US police officer	$300,000
Percentage speeding ticket that get contested in traffic court	5%
Total number of licensed drivers in America today	196,000,000

Top 10 Driving Citation States Rank

1) Ohio
2) Pennsylvania
3) New York
4) California
5) Texas
6) Georgia
7) Virginia
8) North Carolina
9) Massachusetts
10) Connecticut

As we can verify from the official data above, the average percentage of individuals who receive traffic tickets for speed in the USA is only 20.6%. "Coincidentally," that is the percentage of individuals who belong to minority ethnic backgrounds (blacks, Latinos, and Asians), which includes immigrants, legal (who pursue a green card or citizenship) and illegal. And this is an even broader issue, as it reflects the hidden practice of racism by the legal authorities, which is nevertheless illegal. The only advantage that a legal immigrant has is that he/she will, most of the time, not be charged with a crime on their first ticket. Anyway, he/she will be cornered everywhere, may have his/her drivers licence suspended multiple times, and he/she will pay outrageously higher car insurance policies due to his/her "bad driving record." Undocumented immigrants, besides supposedly having committed a civil infraction of the law (speeding, going through a red light, etc), will be charged for the crime of driving without a license. They will be fingerprinted, just like a rapist, murderer, or drug dealer.

The discrimination against minorities and the immigrants is an uncontestable fact if we analyze the statistics and follow real-life cases. As mentioned before, I came to the USA to study with the intention of going back to continue my career in my country. As a graduate student here, although I had a valid international driver's license, I used mostly public transportation, due to the convenience and lower costs. When I got my Connecticut driver's license I started to drive my husband's car, which was relatively new, in good shape, and carried his license's plate.

Two years and a half later, after we moved to Massachusetts, upon my acceptance to attend a master's program in Opera at the Boston Conservatory, our socio-economic situation declined significantly, as the cost of living in Massachusetts is much higher then in Connecticut. My then partner had difficulties finding a job and ended up accepting one with a similar salary he used to make in Connecticut. As a full-time student, I didn't have time to work, and we still needed to pay for child care for my daughter. Our lifestyle was then very modest, and we used public transportation most of the time to save money. In my second year of the master's program, I got a job as the music director of a church in Boston and a few months later I was hired as a bilugual counselor and advocate in a program for victims of domestic violence. My salaries were modest, but our situation improved a little.

Due to a more complex work schedule, we had to buy another car, but it had to be a very affordable used one; we decided to get one that ran well, but was not in good shape aesthetically. The new license plate was now in my name, and that is where all my problems started. Up to then, I had been driving in the USA for around four years, in the states of New York and Connecticut with my partner's car, and my driving record was spotless. Zero tickets. At this point, I was already an American citizen. Shortly after acquiring this "new" car, I started to be stopped by traffic police all the time, and the tickets started to accumulate. I even got a ticket for "ilegal use of horn" after beeping behind another driver, who decided to stop in front of me and a big line of cars on a traffic light, talking on his cell phone, and stayed stopped through multiple red and green lights, making the rush hour traffic even more chaotic. The police officer, instead of asking him to pull over and free the traffic for the other cars, gave me a ticket. The officer was not interested to know that I had a very strict schedule, leaving work and going to pick up my daughter at the daycare, before 6:00 p.m., when the school closed. Do you know anyone who was charged for such a ticket? Now you do, and perhaps some of your immigrant friends have, too. After accumulating five tickets in two years, three of them being for parking (for getting to the meter a few minutes after the time had expired to feed the meter), one for going five miles above the speed limit, and that insane one for "illegal use of horn," I got a letter from the Department of Motor Vehicles, with a notice that I must attend a mandatory retraining in order to avoid suspension of my driver's license.

Those mandatory classes are administered by private companies, which arbitrarily charge very high fees, as the Department of Motor Vehicles outsources those services. Those third-party companies are notorious for their very lucrative profits.

Getting to the course, after paying the $150 application fee in full to assure a seat at this eight-hour retraining, I went to the assigned location, passing through the numerous classrooms of other penalized drivers. I noticed that most of us were minorities. Besides revisiting the Massachusetts traffic laws, that did not differ much to the ones from Connecticut, which I have learned, some comments from the instructor started to resonate with me, being an eye-opener. One of them was the fact that cars with vibrant colors or in visibly bad shape, are more noticeable by the officer, as this is a natural human tendency. Well, the second part fitted my situation perfectly, as this second car didn't look great. But my partner's car that I drove in Connecticut and New York was bright red, and I was never stopped. So far the license plates in different names were the only explanation. The comment was that after the driver gets some tickets, he starts to be targeted for further tickets, as the license plate belongs to the driver, not the car. If you change your car, you have to move your license plate to your new car. So, this driver starts to be seen as a higher-risk driver. That creates a snowball effect of points accumulated, higher insurance costs, and less credibility in court. The red car I used to drive before had his license plate; he was a Caucasian-American. After moving to Massachusetts, a state which coincidentally has the largest concentration of Brazilian Immigrants in America, the second car had my license plate, someone with a very Brazilian last name.

At the end of the course, which took the whole Saturday, the instructor pulled me aside to give me my grades and certificate of completion and whispered in my ear: "Why are you here? You clearly does not fit in the profile of a high-risk or agressive driver! I answered what I believed, without getting into politics—that it was probably because the signage in Massachusetts was very badly made, with very small traffic and street signs, hidden behind trees and buildings or even absent, and I was used to driving in Connecticut and New York were the signage was much better and clear. However, I started to question in my own head, if there was nothing beyond that subtle change, based on the instructor's comments during that course. Today, analyzing the statistics, comparing the records of minorities and the dominant ethnic groups, I am convinced that such discrepancy is not a mere coincidence.

For over a decade, numerous researchers have unanimously proven two very simple and clear facts, related to the relationship between the immigrant and the law:

A) Immigrants are less inclined to commit serious crimes than the native-born citizen of any country.
B) Higher rates of immigration are not associated with higher rates of crimes against property or people.

Despite this scientific data, the American federal government, through President George W. Bush's mandate of 2007, established what is called a "bed quota", through which the federal government guarantees the occupation of 34,000 beds daily in the USA prisons, which costs $2 billion dollars per year! This exorbitant amount is taken from the public budget, from the taxpayers and transferred to the private oligarchies, owners of the incarceration facilities.

Numerous attempts were made by American Senate representatives from both parties (Democrat and Republican) to eliminate this immoral mandate, done solely to benefit this very small but wealthy private sector. It is important to mention that this quota of jail detention would never be approved by the American people and would be the root of protests and lawsuits against the government if the common Caucasian non-immigrant American citizen were the target population for it. The solution for those lobbyists was to criminalize the immigrant. Imagine your city council ordering the police of your town as far as how many people needed to be arrested every day, regardless of whether they had committed a crime. Such logistics have nothing to do with the prevention or punishment of crime, or the assurance of public safety. Pure and simple, this reflects the economic interests of those factions. However, when it comes to detention of immigrants, there are different standards of law.

The university professor Julliett Stumpf named such

phenomena "crimination" – the criminalization of the laws of immigration. The Illegal Immigration Reform and Immigrant Responsibility Act (IIRIRA), as well as the Anti-Terrorism and the Effective Death Penalty Act (AEDPA), transformed immigration laws in two major ways. First, the laws started to enforce the detention and deportation of all non-citizen individuals (legal or not), condemned for a serious crime. Second, the laws established the legal definition of what constitutes a serious crime when it comes to the immigrant, which should be applied for infractions committed in periods much prior to the date this law was created. Therefore, if a permanent resident (immigrant with a green card), was found withholding taxes in 1985, he would be punished with a fine. Today, the government can deport and send him/her to jail. The experts call this discrepancy of weights and measures an error of justice.

Even then, such standards and measures have been in force for a decade and a half and have gotten worse thanks to the "Secure Community Programs" from the USA National Homeland Security (DHS), tailored to detect deportable immigrants in US jails. Under this program, individuals charged with crimes, attempted crimes, or incarcerated have their fingerprints taken and their records are registered and cross-referenced by both the criminal and the immigration archives. If they are not registered at the Immigration Department, they are submitted to the custody of ICE (Immigration and Customs Enforcement).

With no surprise, we notice that the new classes of "criminals," detained by the recently institutionalized crimes of immigration, are not violent individuals and do not represent any risk to public safety in their communities. Anyway, according to those programs that are spreading through the country epidemiologically, more and more immigrants are being detained in American jails before being deported.

The detention and deportation machine also feeds through law enforcement at American borders, capturing immigrants in large groups, who cross the border without a visa. Such individuals are captured and incarcerated in cells kept at very low temperatures (called ice boxes) and left there under inhumane conditions.

Families being unnecessarily separated, millions of immigrants being tortured with a life lived in paranoia and trauma, millions dying in the Mexican deserts and mountains, trying to return to the USA to be reunited with their families in the USA...these are all tragedies that could be avoided with a little injection of humanity into the system and American immigration laws, which serve not the community and the American collective interests, but the greed of the penitentiary industry, whose fortune leaves the public treasure, landing in the pockets of this insignificant but wealthy and powerful group, the owners of for-profit jails.

The two major penitentiary corporations are the GEO, Inc Group with its administrative headquarters in Boca Raton, Florida, serving the USA, making a fortune of $1.61 billion and a net profit of $77.5 million in 2011. The second is the Correction Corporation of America (CCA), with its administrative headquarters in Nashville, TN, which accumulated a fortune of $1.76 billion and collected a net profit of $162.51 million in 2011. Those and other penitentiary private corporations spend large sums in bribes to legislators, to get them to create and approve absurd laws of immigration such as SB1070 of Arizona, with the only goal of maintaining their billionaire profits.

The first agreement of CCA with the government took place in 1983, under President Reagan's government, when the privatization and mass detention gave birth to the penitentiary industry complex. Laws assured the minimum detention quota and the increase of the incarceration time for sentences of nonviolent drug crimes. At the end of the '90s, when the American economy reached its summit, crime levels significantly fell and the penitentiary corporations almost reached bankrupcy. The terrorist attacks of 9/11 under President Bush and at the beginning of President Obama's government came "in good time" to those sectors, since that gave them an excuse to create the programs and modifications of the immigration laws. Since then, such corporations' profits exploded, and they are expanding their empire with the construction of new facilities.

Besides those companies, there are many others associated with the penitentiary industry, who are contracted to deliver third-party services of meal supplies, medical and dental assistance, and telephone services to the inmates, all sponsored by public money. More people incarcerated means higher profits to those corporations and the easy target are the immigrants, legal and illegal.

Illegal immigrants need to be incarcerated? Both the data related from public safety and the numbers clearly show that they do not. Other methods such as GPS tracking would cost the public budget around $ 8/day, and each inmate costs $ 119/day from financial resources from your taxes.

The question that arises then is: Do such immigration laws serve the American citizen taxpayers, or merely the greed of the 1% of the population, who retains the accumulated economic power?

Reverend John Fife was convicted in 1986 for sheltering desperate immigrants from South America who were fleeing from the civil wars in their countries. He said: "If the American government will not recognize those people fleeing from the brutal attacks of the deadly squads and massacres of villages in South America as refugees, we have no ethical choice but to help them not to get caught by the USA immigration and police. For them, being captured would be a life sentence. So, as humane people and Christians we have this moral obligation to shelter them." His initiative gave birth to what is now known as the Sanctuary in Tucson, Arizona. He and eight other people involved in this mission were sentenced to five years' probation in the scheme to smuggle Central and South Americans into the USA, in the Sanctuary case.

Reverend Alison Harrington, pastor of Southside Presbyterian Church and one of the leaders of the Sanctuary nowadays in Tucson, Arizona said: "Upon the failure of political leadership, religious leaderships are arising to advocate and to protect the victims of the war against immigrants."

There are currently around 11.7 million undocumented immigrants from all parts of the world in America. 60% of them attend church at least twice a month. They are parents and represent 5.2% of the workforce in America. If all of them were to be deported, we would have 4.5 million children missing at least one parent. Three hundred and seventy thousand individuals were removed from this country last year only for being undocumented immigrants. America spends 18 billion tax dollars per year to enforce border security. It's more than the budgets of the FBI and CIA combined! The current immigration laws treat mothers, fathers, and honest workers as felons and potentially kills 300 to 500 mothers and fathers, who are also workers, per year.

Some church and other non-religious community

organizations, as well as legislators from both the Republican and the Democratic parties, have been fighting for decades to stop the militarization of immigration and to pass humane immigration laws through much-needed Immigration Reform, which would prioritize families and not separate them. However, with the economic growth of the incarceration industry, the lobbyists continue to spend outrageous sums of cash to avoid the reform, as this would represent the breakage of their beyond-lucrative fountain of gold.

An article published by the American Immigration Council states: "Catholic Legal Immigration Network (CLINIC), the American Immigration Council, Refugee and Immigrant Center for Education and Legal Services (RAICES), and the American Immigration Lawyers Association (AILA), partners in the CARA Family Detention Pro Bono Project, are calling on the government to fully comply with US District Court Judge Dolly Gee's ruling concerning the inhumane incarceration of mothers and children fleeing violence and persecution."

For over a year, the federal government has neglected the *Flores* Settlement Agreement, which, for nearly two decades, set the binding minimum standards for the detention and treatment of immigrant children. The court ordered the government on July 24 and August 21, 2015 to provide remedies to the problem by October 23, 2015. Although the government has appealed that decision, it did not request a stay of the order. Thus, the court's ruling stands as the appeal moves forward, and as of today, children should be released "without unnecessary delay."

As of October 23, 2015, the CARA Project's data indicates that approximately 195 families represented by them have been confined in family detention facilities in Texas for more than twenty days. The number of client families detained for longer than five days is even higher. It is estimated that 507 families, represented by the CARA Project, have been detained for more than five days. These numbers include only family units represented by the CARA Project, so the numbers of children and mothers held in violation of the *Flores* ruling is likely significantly higher.

The Department of Homeland Security has not taken the steps necessary to comply with the court order. Moreover, its attempts to fast-track state licensing of the Texas facilities and to coerce mothers into accepting ankle monitors without their attorneys present, as well as the continuing deplorable medical care, show that they are betting everything on the success of an appeal to the court's order.

Considering that the health and well-being of thousands of children and their mothers is at stake, the government's continuing policy of detaining families is a slap in the face to judicial authority and our nation's values. (released October 23, 2015)

Other reports published at the American Immigration Council say: "For more than a century, innumerable studies have confirmed two simple yet powerful truths about the relationship between immigration and crime: immigrants are less likely to commit serious crimes or be behind bars than the native-born, and high rates of immigration are associated with lower rates of violent crime and property crime. This holds true for both legal immigrants and the unauthorized, regardless of their country of origin or level of education. In other words, the overwhelming majority of <u>immigrants</u> <u>are not criminals</u> by any commonly accepted definition of the term. For this reason, harsh immigration policies are not effective in fighting crime. Unfortunately, immigration policy is frequently shaped more by fear and stereotype than by empirical evidence. As a result, immigrants have the stigma of 'criminality' ascribed to them by an ever-evolving assortment of laws and immigration-enforcement mechanisms. Put differently, immigrants are being defined more and more as threats. Whole new classes of 'felonies' have been created which apply only to immigrants, deportation has become a punishment for even minor offenses, and policies aimed at trying to end unauthorized immigration have been made more punitive rather than more rational and practical. In short, immigrants themselves are being criminalized."

Immigrants are *Less* Likely to be Criminals Than the Native-Born Higher Immigration Is Associated with Lower Crime Rates

- Between 1990 and 2013, the foreign-born share of the US population grew from 7.9 % to 13.1 % and the number of unauthorized immigrants more than tripled from 3.5 million to 11.2 million.
- During the same period, FBI data indicate that the violent crime rate declined 48 %—which included falling rates of aggravated assault, robbery, rape, and murder. Likewise, the property crime rate fell 41 %, including declining rates of motor vehicle theft, larceny/robbery, and burglary.

Immigrants Are Less Likely than the Native-Born to Be Behind Bars

- According to an original analysis of data from the 2010 American Community Survey (ACS) conducted by the authors of this report, roughly 1.6 % of immigrant males age 18-39 are incarcerated, compared to 3.3 % of the native-born. This disparity in incarceration rates has existed for decades, as evidenced by data from the 1980, 1990, and 2000 decennial censuses. In each of those years, the incarceration rates of the native-born were anywhere from two to five times higher than that of immigrants.
- The 2010 census data reveals that incarceration rates among the young, less-educated Mexican,

Salvadoran, and Guatemalan men who make up the bulk of the unauthorized population are significantly lower than the incarceration rate among native-born young men without a high-school diploma. In 2010, less-educated native-born men age 18-39 had an incarceration rate of 10.7 %—more than triple then the 2.8 % rate among foreign-born Mexican men, and five times greater than the 1.7 % rate among foreign-born Salvadoran and Guatemalan men.

Immigrants Are Less Likely Than the Native-Born to Engage in Criminal Behavior

A variety of different studies using different methodologies has found that immigrants are less likely than the native-born to engage in either violent or nonviolent "antisocial" behaviors; that immigrants are less likely than the native-born to be repeat offenders among "high risk" adolescents; and that immigrant youth who were students in US middle and high schools in the mid-1990s and are now young adults have among the lowest delinquency rates of all young people.

Despite the abundance of evidence that immigration is not linked to higher crime rates, and that immigrants are less likely to be criminals than the native-born, many US policymakers succumb to their fears and prejudices about what they imagine immigrants to be. As a result, far too many immigration policies are drafted on the basis of stereotypes rather than substance. These laws are criminalizing an ever- broadening swath of the immigrant population by applying a double standard when it comes to consequences for criminal behavior. Immigrants who experience even the slightest brush with the criminal justice system, such as being convicted of a misdemeanor, can find themselves subject to detention for an undetermined period, after which they are expelled from the country and barred from returning. In other words, for years the government has been redefining what it means to be a "criminal alien," using increasingly stringent definitions and standards of "criminality" that do not apply to US citizens.

Of course, these increasingly punitive laws are only as effective as the immigration-enforcement apparatus designed to support them. And this apparatus has expanded dramatically over the past three decades. More and more immigrants have been smashed by law enforcement mechanisms new and old, from worksite raids to Secure Communities. Detained immigrants are then housed in a growing nationwide network of private, for-profit prisons before they are deported from the United States. In short, as US immigration laws create more and more "criminal aliens," the machinery of detention and deportation grows larger as well, casting a widening dragnet over the nation's foreign-born population in search of anyone who might be deportable. With the technologically sophisticated enforcement systems in place today, being stopped by a police officer for driving a car with a broken tail light can culminate in a one-way trip out of the country if the driver long ago pled guilty to a misdemeanor that has since been defined as a deportable offense.

The scale of the federal government's drive to criminalize immigration and expand the reach of the enforcement dragnet becomes very apparent when the proliferation of immigration laws, policies, and enforcement mechanisms is tracked over the past three decades. Two bills passed by Congress in 1996 stand as the most flagrant modern examples of laws which create a system of justice for non-US citizens that is distinct from the system that applies to citizens. From old-fashioned worksite raids to the modern databases at the heart of initiatives such as Secure Communities and the Criminal Alien Program (CAP), the government's immigration-enforcement mechanisms continue to expand and reach deeper and deeper into the immigrant community. In the process, basic principles of fairness and equal treatment under the law are frequently left by the wayside. (Edwing, Martinez, Rumbault, 2015)

CASES OF IMMIGRANTS

C.C.

C. immigrated from Brazil to the USA, in search of a better life. In the USA he met and married an American citizen woman in the state of Massachusetts, who had a daughter from a previous marriage. C.

learned to love and care for that child as his own. After having his green card approved, they all went to Brazil to visit his family and to consolidate their marriage in the presence of his family and friends. On the way back home, he was detained at the American airport and deported to Brazil, being separated from his wife and daughter. Worried about his wife, who was unable to take care of herself and her daughter alone, C. unsuccessfully tried to appeal to the authorities. Without the support of the legal system, he adventured through the borders of Mexico. At this point the circumstances had become much more strict for immigrants, due to the changes in American immigration policies and laws. The conservative media, taking advantage of the tragic circumstances of terrorist attacks, was bombarding the news with crimes allegedly committed by minorities and immigrants. In a country built on disagreements, conflicts, and wars, this is more than sufficient to install a collective and generalized aversion to immigrants, who are seen and treated as suspects, creating discrimination even in places and circumstances where those dynamics were absent or imperceptible.

C. gladly managed to come back and was once again taking good care of his wife and daughter, doing it with pleasure. He continued to be the hardworking, honest, and caring person he had always been. However, their joy didn't last long. He was caught once again by the immigration and sent to jail in Massachusetts. His wife visited him frequently at the detention unit.

He refused to sign the deportation letter, as he would not be able to take care of his wife and daughter while living in Brazil. There, he would not have the means, without any professional training, to guarantee financial support to his family in the USA. He knew his teenaged daughter would not adjust well to the lifestyle in Brazil. She indeed refused to move there with her parents. As a coercive strategy, the immigration authorities transferred him to another detention unit in New Hampshire, farther from home. His wife visited him less frequently, due to the four-hour drive and difficulties accomodating the longer commute in her schedule.

Aside from the greater distance from his family, at the New Hampshire detention center, the policies and conditions there were reportedly harder for him.

Immigration inmates share the same space with dangerous criminals. This in itself reflects the mentality of the local culture in regard to immigrants. He has also described several incidents were he was allegedly abused and discriminated against by police officers and staff there.

One day, after a meal in the cafeteria, he reported opening the container of juice given to everyone with the meal, to take his prescribed pills for high blood pressure and diabetes. The police officer reportedly saw it and reprimanded him for doing it, saying that pills could only be taken with water, not with juice. He was confused because he had never heard anything like that from his doctor. For a moment, he was trying to figure out how he would do it, as they did not give them any water and reportedly they were not allowed to help themselves in the kitchen or faucet. Since he needed to take his meds at that time, he decided to swallow the pills without any liquid, to avoid problems with the officer. Right after, he reportedly observed another inmate, a Caucasian American man, who was seating at another table besides his, opening his own container of juice and taking his pills with it. Perplexed, he respectfully asked the officer why the other man could do it and he couldn't. The officer "answered" by reportedly dragging him to a solitary confinement for two days, which just confirmed the alleged arbitrary nature of the rules, the abuse of power, and lack of ethics of the officer.

He reportedly stayed at the New Hampshire detention center for three or four months, transferred abruptly to Alabama, and then sent back to Massachusetts. He reportedly continued to bounce back and forth from prison to prison for 20 months to this day.

S.M.

S. came to America from Brazil over twenty years ago, with his wife and their two-year-old daughter, as his wife wanted to adventure into a new beginning after her father died. In Brazil, he used to work as a writer and editor for a local newspaper at his hometown in Minas Gerais. His responsibilities were broad, his work schedule prolonged, and his budget tight.

Here, he soon found jobs and lived an impecable life for years, working honestly, paying taxes, raising their daughter, and helping everyone around them. His criminal record was nonexistent, his credit was excellent, and they were genuinely good people. After years of a marriage that was already problematic since they left Brazil, the couple decided to get divorced. His wife has never recovered from the loss of her father, which affected her ability to open up for a happy life with her partner. Even though he knew that this outcome was inevitable, S. fell into a deep depression. But he still managed to go to Brazil and take care of the divorce there, as the Brazilian laws required. A few years later, he met another woman, an American citizen, and years later they applied for his green card in the state of New Hampshire, where she resided. Upon marriage, the couple decided that S. would stay during the week in a room in Massachusetts and on the weekend he would go home to New Hampshire, as this would save them a significant sum of money in gas, and time in commute from that remote location in New Hampshire to his work place. The wife could not move to Massachusetts at that time, as she was living in New Hampshire to take care of her elderly and disabled cousin.

During the green card process, the immigration officer responsible for his case accused them of a fraudulent marriage, since S. would spend the week in Massachusetts and his wife in New Hampshire. Regardless of the numerous evidence, the testimonies of friends and family members that they were a legit couple, they continued to feel pressured by the officer so he decided to move permanently to New Hampshire and commute every day to work, as there were no jobs available in that state for him. He needed to travel for four to five hours a day, each way, to and from work. The couple as well as S.'s ex-wife allegedly received multiple unscheduled visits, without prior notices, from the New Hampshire immigration staff, looking for something that proved that S.'s second marriage was a fraud. His ex-wife resided with their daughter in Massachusetts. They never found anything. Four years later into the application process, after two successful interviews, two attorneys, a very tall pile of documents required by the immigration department and impeccably delivered by their attorneys, with absolutely no evidence to sustain their fraud allegation, his case is left inconclusive for five years, solely due to the alleged prejudice of the immigration officer responsible for his case and considering the numerous reports from other New Hampshire cases, due to the alleged extreme prejudice and racist immigration policies of that state.

His attorney, reportedly one of the best in the field, tried unsuccessfully to have an appointment with that officer, who reportedly expresses deliberate lack of effort to find a conclusion to the case. She could not deny his green card as there is no evidence against the legitimacy of their marriage, therefore, her attitude has been allegedly described as pure abuse of power and racism, deeply affecting several people's lives. Their lives continued to be in suspense, unable to make any further plans, professionally and personally, before his case is concluded. S., his current wife, and his ex-wife's mental health are deeply affected at this point. His ex-wife is suffering because of the random visits and harassments by the New Hampshire immigration stuff, and the couple is suffering for the same reason along with the stress of having their lives stuck. They are all presenting strong symptoms of anxiety and depression, being in treatment. His ex-wife is also in treatment for high blood pressure, a problem she reportedly never had before, triggered by the invasions to her house and the harassment she is reportedly suffering from those immigration officers.

C.L.

C. crossed the border, coming from Mexico to the USA with her three children. For years she lived safely in Douglas, Arizona with her children, working in the church, caring and providing for herself and for them. One day, she went to pick up her daughter at school and on her way back she was stopped by a police officer. He allegedly said, "You were going too fast."

She replied, "Sorry, sir, but this is not possible as I was following traffic and I was right behind you."

He asked for her driver's license. She handled him her Mexican's driver's license, as it was the only one she had. He allegedly said, "You don't have documents to live here, do you?

She honestly answered, "No, but please do not call Immigration on me." Her daughters also started to cry and begged him not to send her mother away from them.

The police officer coldly said, "You are going back to Mexico." After several weeks in detention, thanks to funds raised by her church, C. was released and a court date on her deportation is still pending. Her church family in Douglas stands with her.

L.R.

L. was a nineteen-year-old Mexican woman found by a couple driving by, right in the crossing from Mexico to the USA. She was fleeing away from domestic violence with her seventeen-month-old baby girl. She ran short of water and started to give all the water to her baby. She died of dehydration shortly after, and her baby survived.

M.V.

M. is a mother of three children and lived for many years in Tucson, Arizona with them. Three years ago she learned the news that her sister had been murdered by her husband, as a victim of domestic violence. She was devastated and needed to go back to Mexico to give her nephews and family some emotional and financial support.

After a few months living there, she realized that

the violence and economic situation were even worse than when she left the first time, making it nearly impossible for her to provide for her family. She borrowed some money and tried to cross the borders with the coyotes. They told her it would be a short walk, but it was far longer and more difficult than she had been informed. She felt she couldn't physically do it, but she kept going. Following the instructions remotely given by the coyote on her phone, she stopped and hid by some bushes. The coyote told her to hide and wait as he would pick her up shortly. After fifty minutes of waiting, she heard the sound of horses getting closer. Not having anywhere else to run and hide, she stayed there and was caught by the border police on horses, and sent to detention and back to Mexico. She is still struggling to survive with her kids, and plans to try again as she reportedly has no other choice to provide for her kids. Besides the deep psychological, economic and physical struggles M. has had and still faces throughout this processes, she suffers tremendous guilt for being an honest person, but needing to do something considered illegal, crossing the border to the USA and being sent to jail. She has also forgiven herself many times, as she knows she has no choice in order to provide for her children.

B.T.

B. came to the USA for the first time at the age of ten, with her parents, who were accepted for a fellowship program in Veterinary Medicine at the University of Colorado. The parents successfully completed their fellowship and returned to Brazil for their well-established and honorable careers. Due to their excellent performance and academic accomplishments, the father was invited by the university to return and work there as a researcher and faculty. After some reluctance, the couple decided to accept the offer and moved back to the USA in 2008. B. was starting high school, so she adjusted well to life in America and through her father's work contract, the whole family got a green card. Every year, B. would go to Brazil to visit her family, sometimes with her parents, sometimes with relatives who would come to visit them. Years later, during her first year of college, she went to visit her family during summer break and on her way back she was happy with the good times in Brazil, excited to return to her loving parents and for another year in college. Her flight had a scheduled stop in Texas and she was taken by the police upon arrival in the airport. She was held hostage there for hours, without explanation from anyone as to why she was being detained. She kept asking the guards and staff, saying she had a valid green card, therefore it must be some kind of mistake. They were reportedly rude and kept telling her to shush. She was then transferred to the detention center in Texas, together with other people. She continued to ask other staff and officers what was the basis for her detention, but no answer.

Upon arrival, she and the other women were placed in an "ice box" (jail cells set with an icy cold room temperature), as a method to coerce them into signing deportation papers, and for torture. Day in and day out she kept asking people for clarification, feeling very confused by the whole situation. During all that time, she and the other immigrant allegedly had both their Miranda rights and their Section 23 rights violated by the authorities. After weeks, she was told that her arrest was related to an incident she had in her record, when a traffic police stopped her and they found a cannabis pipe in her trunk. Even though she was found innocent, as the pipe belonged to her American college friend, who was taking a ride with her that day, they used the incident to justify that allegedly abusive and unlawful detention. She then notified her parents, who provided her with a good attorney and after twenty-eight days she was reportedly released, and her case dismissed. She was traumatized by the experience, but she was not entitled to any compensation for the alleged violation of her civil rights, abuse and violence suffered there.

F.I.

F. is a father of two small children. One day after the birth of his second child, F. was detained by immigration agents and sent to an incarceration unit in Massachusetts for one misdemeanor. According to Homeland Security's own criteria, he should not be considered priority for detention or deportation. In addition, he is allegedly having his rights of Parental Accountability (DAPA--deferred by President Obama) violated, since his children are both US citizens. F. has been in the USA since he was sixteen years old and has made this country his home. His entire family lives in the USA. His wife had to move with their two daughters to a relative's home, because they were no longer able to pay rent and other expenses. His wife and daughters needed psychological treatment due to the trauma caused by F.' s detention and possible deportation.

L.S.

This thirty-year-old man has lived in the USA for almost twenty years, and has three small children and a wife. Early in 2015, he allegedly was wrongly charged with robbery by a police officer in Georgia, without having the opportunity to clarify or to defend himself. In October he was declared innocent, but instead of being released, he was placed on immigration hold and sent to immigration detention. ICE is insisting to send F. to deportation, leaving his wife and three children here without a husband and a father. There is no evidence that he represent any danger to society, and he also had been initially detained allegedly in violation of his Miranda and Section 23 rights of persons arrested or detained.

O.J.

The father of two children, O. came to the USA in 1998, running from extreme violence and danger to his life in South America. He met an American citizen, whom he married. One day, during a routine police call, O. answered the door at his place. Without knowing his name or if he lived there, he was allegedly assaulted by the police, accused of obstruction of justice, and had his back injured by the incident. He was taken to the hospital ER and after examination, he was strongly recommended to proceed to surgery. ICE allegedly took him to detention instead. He is being refused his prescribed medication, to be granted humanitarian medical leave, or to be granted his persecutory discretion. He reportedly continues to be in excruciating pain, without medication or medical treatment, and detained for committing a misdemeanor, which is not eligible for incarceration to an American-born citizen. O. is a husband, father, hard worker, and a legal permanent resident of the USA.

C.A.

C. was in his late thirties when he came from São Paulo to the USA with his wife and four children. He worked and lived in Massachusetts for over a decade, and was able to build some assets. He felt he was stable enough to start a business back in Brazil and enjoy a good life back there with his immediate and extended families. Things didn't work as expected and a couple of years after the move, he was broken and decided to come back to the USA to start over. The hardships of losing everything, being older, and with the responsability of providing for the family was too much for him--he became deeply depressed, but refused to engage in psychotherapy. C. was found by his wife coming back from the grocery store, in his room hanged by a rope from the ceiling. He left a deep trauma in all his family and friends.

SECTION 23 of RIGHTS OF PERSONS ARRESTED OR DETAINED

Section 23 of the Bill of Rights Act states that:

- Everyone who is arrested or who is detained under any enactment:
- Shall be informed at the time of the arrest or detention of the reason for it and
- Shall have the right to counsel and instruct a lawyer without delay and to be informed of that right; and
- Shall have the right to have the validity of the arrest and detention determined without delay by way of habeas corpus and to be released if the arrest or detention is not lawful.

2) Everyone who is arrested or who is detained under any enactment:

3) Everyone who is arrested for an offense and is not released shall be brought as soon as possible before a court or competente tribunal.

4) Everyone who is arrested or detained under any

enactment for any offense or suspected offense shall have the right to refrain from making any statement and to be informed of that right.

Everyone deprived of liberty shall be treated with humanity and with respect for the inherent dignity of the person.

7

THE IMMIGRANT: ADJUSTMENT AND MENTAL HEALTH

The migratory experience can be traumatic due to several factors.

a) The first is a single traumatic event—there have been many cases reported to me in the clinic in which the individuals were victims of rape, by the "coyotes" (Mexicans whose illegal job is to facilitate and transport the immigrants through the borders of Mexico to USA) or by gangs who attack and take advantage of the individual trying to cross the border. Rape is so common that many women report taking contraceptive pills months before their scheduled trip to cross the borders through Mexico. Taking advantage of the potential immigrants' vulnerability and dependence, being 100% in their hands without absolutely no civil or legal rights from anywhere, those coyotes act arbitrarily and sometimes with brutality, raping women in front of their children, who are held hostage with military guns. Sometimes, they are raped during the long walk through deserted areas in Mexico, if they are not in groups. Interestingly, many of those roads and areas have radars and cameras installed by the police to capture the undocumented potential immigrants. They capture many of those who are alone or even in groups, but no report is made that any law enforcement ever showed up in those same locations during a rape to save the women. Even the ones who have the good luck not to face the rapist coyotes can be victims of other common types of abuse, such as verbal or financial, taking all their money, beyond the highly expensive fees they had to pay in advance in order to receive their services in the first place. Those fees are around $4,000 to $15,000 dollars per person, paid up front and in full upon scheduling of the passage, which takes several days or weeks.

The long walk by land, or transport in the trunks of cars or trucks, through the Mexican and Texan deserts, under very high temperatures during the day and intense cold at night, without access to water or food, make their feet covered with blisters that look like third degree burns, and lead many to faint, consequently getting very sick with dehydration, infections, being bitten by poisonous snakes and scorpions, fractures, etc. Those are left to die in the desert, without money or water, and obviously without any medical assistance.

b) The second type of traumas are the ones acquired through the accumulation of negative experiences associated with the condition of the immigrants' lives, and cultural shock, which triggers the deterioration of the immigrant's mental and physical health. The stress, the social isolation, precarious living situations, poor eating schedule and quality, sleep deprivation, climate and cultural shock, as well as professional and personal dissatisfaction, accumulate and slowly cause the deterioration of the immigrant's health to the point of losing their identity, sense of personal value, and meaning of life.

This is a very common occurence among the ones whose only objective is the accumulation of assets in their country of origin. They subject themselves to extremely long working hours, problematic and depriving housing conditions, gathering in large groups of strangers in one house and sharing the space without much privacy or comfort to minimize their expenses, depriving themselves of leisure, social life, cultural events, personal, medical or dental care, sustaining for years their only goal of buying or building a house back in their country or starting their own business. Many of those cases, however, involve individuals with low education, and little or no business or real estate experience. Besides, many of them are victims of dishonest and unscrupulous family members back in their country, who steal and divert their money, pretending to follow requests for investment or business management. Many cases are documented (fortunately none were my clients), where the immigrants committed suicide after years and years of self-deprivation and very hard work, realizing that all their money was lost or stolen and they ended up with nothing--no money, no housing, no real estate, no business. Along with the tragedy of losing their lives, their spouses and children were left sometimes with debts, and certainly severe traumas.

Through the accumulation of common, small negative events, the individual therefore can lose their identity or life. One of the most important aspects that triggers emotional decompensation is the insane level of stress from the heavy work load, lack of sleep, social isolation, and self-deprivation combined.

The children of immigrants also suffer with the dysfunction and deprivation of their parents' lives. The most common disorders among children and adolescents from first-generation immigrant parents are depression, anxiety, panic disorder, phobias, eating disorders, and behavioral issues. All of those disorders affect, one way or another, their academic performance or social adjustment at school, which lead their schools to contact the parents and recomment psychological treatment.

The families whose parents present higher levels of education (high school or above), are able sometimes to detect their children's issues by themselves and look for bilingual professional help, to assist them with parenting skills, as well as social and cultural adjustment for the whole family.

Some others do not realize that their children are being negatively affected until their problems escalate to serious academic or behavioral problems, involvement with drugs or aggressiveness, most commonly toward themselves (self-mutilation, eating disorders, or attempted suicide).

The alienation of the Brazilian community in regard to reaching professional psychological help is aggravated by the absence of health insurance for the undocumented immigrant, which makes them avoid even more reaching for professional help for self and their children, due to the higher costs and the fear of deportation. Free medical assistance programs were installed in some states, such as Massachusetts, and there are also some religious or non-profit organizations that offer basic medical care to individuals without health insurance.

Many of them seek social services and support from religious institutions. Some of those institutions do this work responsibly, hiring health professionals who volunteer their services, providing medical and psychological care as well as informative and educational workshops. Sometimes those professionals are paid through fundraising and grants. Other services, however, are provided by priests with inadequate education, sharing distorted and unethical values, discouraging their communities from reaching for medical and psychological treatments, an attitude that promotes the increase of alienation and symptoms. The illegal immigrants' fear of being reported to ICE and deported also contributes to their alienation in regard to health care—even in extreme cases of domestic violence perpetrated by their American or foreign husbands—and clinical depression. The individuals opt to remain in unsafe and unhealthy circumstances, believing there are no alternatives.

Although awareness of those issues has slightly improved in the last years, through radio station campaigns, services provided by philanthropic institutions, and the Brazilian Consulate initiatives, much still needs to be done to promote better levels of health and social assistance to immigrants in the USA in general.

Social adjustment represents an important part of the achievement and maintenance of mental health. In studies of cultural shock and acculturation, multiple authors describe the ways in which the immigrant individual experiences this process in a more positive or negative manner. Results depend on factors such as loneliness (Pruitt, 1978), satisfaction in marriage (Naidoo, 1985), levels of stress experienced during the cross-cultural process (Spandley e Phillips, 1972), and work status (Chung e Kagawa-Singer, 1993; MacCarthy e Craissati, 1989; Nwadiora e McAdoo, 1996).

The number of immigrants and refugees settling in the USA has increased in the last decades. The overwhelming majority of children in immigrant families (88 % in 2013) are US-born. The Migration Policy Institute's tabulation of data from the US Census Bureau's 2013 American Community Survey and 1990 Census decennial data, shows that in 1990, 13.4% of the US born children belong to first generation immigrant families (who's parents, at least one, is residing in the USA, but was born in another country). In 2013 the percentage of US born children from immigrant families raised to 24.9%. In the state of Massachusetts those numbers are: 15.5% in 1990 and 27.3% in 2013. In New York state they count for 23.8% in 1990 and 33.0% in 2013. In Texas they were 19.9% in 1990 and 34.0% in 2013. In Florida there were 19.7 in 1990 and 32.6% in 2013. In Arizona there were 15.7% and

29.0% in 2013. In California they were 38.4% in 1990 and 49.3% in 2013.

This population of parents, at all sources, includes naturalized citizens, lawful permanent residents (LPRs), certain legal non-immigrants (e.g., persons on student or work visas), those admitted under refugee or asylum status, and persons illegally residing in the United States.

Within the current immigration policy, many parents of USA citizen children are being deported to their original countries, as we could see through some of the cases described before. Nearly 4 million total deportations and ½ million were parents of US citizen children. According to the official data from the Migration Policy Institute, there is an estimate of 5.3 million children living with unauthorized immigrant parents in the USA. "Between 2003 and 2013, the U.S. government formally removed 3.7 million immigrants to their home countries. According to the most reliable estimates, parents of U.S.-born children made up between one-fifth and one-quarter of this total." This severely affects their children's mental and physical health, behavior, well-being, overall life outcome, and life integrity.

Children have strong negative psychological reactions to the apprehension, detention, and deportation of their parents. In prior research, subjects described a wide range of mental, physical, and behavioral conditions afflicting children with detained or deported parents (Capps, Chaudry, Castañeda, and Santos 2007; Chaudry et al. 2010; Dreby 2010, 2012; Brabeck and Xu 2010). Participants in the current study reported that children often developed similar problems and lashed out at the parent who was not detained, or at others in school. Most often, children with a detained or deported parent became depressed, which led to deteriorating physical health and performance in school. Study participants reported that children refused to eat, pulled out their hair, or had persistent stomachaches or headaches. Others turned to more self-destructive outlets such as cutting themselves, or substance abuse. Many children lost interest in their daily activities and struggled to maintain positive relationships with their non-detained parent or new guardian. Non-detained parents often suffer from depression after their spouse's detention, which further strains the parent-child relationship. Previous research suggests that depressed parents have more difficulty supporting the healthy development of their children, leading to risks of poor cognitive and behavioral outcomes (Beardslee et al. 1996; Goodman et al. 2011). Research focusing on children with unauthorized immigrant parents has linked parents' unauthorized status to depression and social isolation, which are in turn associated with lower scores on measures of young children's cognitive and socioemotional development (Yoshikawa 2011).

With a parent's deportation, there are negative effects including psychological trauma, material hardship, residential instability, family dissolution, increased use of public benefits, and, among boys, aggression. At the extreme end, some families became permanently separated as parents lose custody or contact with their children.

With all those problems created by the current immigration policies, the federal government faces numerous barriers to meeting the needs of children with deported or detained parents. Studies reported that the difficulties include lack of access to many of the benefits that low-income families might rely on during an economic crisis; lack of access to health care; short supply of key support services that children needed during parental detention or deportation; lack of transportation to access services; social service agencies' lack of resources and experience serving children with deported or detained parents; and difficulties encountered by the child welfare system in coordinating services.

Following parental detention or deportation, most families faced an immediate need for financial support. Children with unauthorized immigrant parents, however, were not always able to receive the public benefits for which they were eligible. Federal legislation bars unauthorized immigrants from participating in major means-tested programs, including Temporary Assistance for Needy Families (TANF), the Supplemental Nutrition Assistance Program (SNAP), Medicaid, and the Children's Health Insurance Program

(CHIP). Therefore, even if they have eligible US-citizen children, families with unauthorized immigrant parents generally receive lower total benefit amounts. For example, SNAP benefits are prorated by the number of eligible individuals in the household. Similarly, TANF benefits are not provided to unauthorized immigrant parents. Consequently, citizen children with unauthorized immigrant parents generally receive lower, "child-only" benefits. In a prior study, unauthorized immigrants had difficulty documenting their income, which is necessary for benefit applications, as a result of off-the-books employment (Speiglman, Castañeda, Brown, and Capps 2013).

PART 2 –
MEMOIRS AND
REFLECTIONS

1

THE SAGA

As mentioned in the introduction, my own experience as an immigrant will be presented here as an useful tool to understand the collective experience of the immigrant. Therefore, with didactic and illustrative purposes to demonstrate the psychological phenomena of the acculturation process, I will describe some experiences related to the phenomenon of immigration, and the psychological and cultural adjustments of my life in America.

Many readers expect to find the confirmation of stereotypes, based on prejudice and discriminatory processes, perpetrated through the local culture. Many hope to find sad stories, involving origins in misery, poverty, and degrading life conditions, inhuman and underdeveloped realities, which make them feel better and superior about their own lives, in comparison to the "under-privileged," when in fact their own lives are experienced as sad, frustrating, and undervalued.

Unfortunately for them, that will not be the case here.

I was fortunate to have built a stable life in Brazil prior to coming to the USA, working as a psychologist and professional classical singer at the São Paulo State Symphonic Orchestra. As it is the case with many, my move to the USA was related to graduate studies, with the intention of going back to Brazil, to my three jobs, upon completion of the master's degree program. I loved my life in Brazil, and despite achieving a comfortable life in the USA, I never again experienced as much happiness as I did through my childhood and youth life in my country. The warmth of the people, the freedom of expression, the comfort of "belonging" to your environment, social context and culture—all are priceless gifts.

I had a comfortable middle-class life with my family there, and contrary to the distorted ideas that some people have about Brazil, most Brazilians (including me) never lived in favelas, never lived in hunger or misery, have never been homeless. (You have no idea how many times I have heard such absurd assumptions about my life there!) Besides of the comfort of having all my needs fulfilled, I was surrounded by happiness from family and friends in cultural consonance, and was privileged to attend excellent colleges and have access to success and growth.

Many immigrants from all over the world leave their homes for financial reasons, in search of better opportunities and quality of life, but that was not my case, which caused me difficulties adjusting to my new life here. I used to repeat constantly to myself: "It will be for a short time; two years will go fast."

But life brings us surprises sometimes, and things do not always go as planned. At a barbecue party, to which I was practically dragged by my roommate friends, I met an American guy, whom I ended up marrying, and with whom I had a daughter. By then, I was oblivious to what this would entail in regard to my identity and all the losses and challenges this would cause in my life. As with most people in this kind of situation, I had in mind the adjustments related to climate, communication, culture, diet, and building a family—the factors that are obvious about life in another country and my new reality. But I imagined nothing even close to the actual reality of things, meaning the cost of this process to my identity and mental health.

Prior to concluding my master's program in music therapy, I decided to take a break from my studies to take care of my baby and family. When my daughter was ready to attend preschool, about three years old, I resumed graduate school. With that, the years were passing and the challenges of resuming my career in Brazil increasing. I made some friends, most of them in similar situations--graduate students, immigrants, or professionals in cultural or academic exchanges. The few American friends I had were individuals with experience living abroad, and therefore, knowledge-able about what it means to be far from your culture, customs, and people.

Even then, little by little, the weight of this reality started to accumulate. Day after day, the social isolation, the depression, the decrease of energy, the weight gain, the premature aging of my face started to interfere with my functionality. I used to look in the mirror and fail to recognize the image reflected there. It was as if the new atmosphere, environment, culture, diet, lifestyle were permeated by a toxic gas, poisoning my essence. I couldn't see myself in there. Who was that person I was seeing in the mirror? What was her identity, personality, values, essence? Nothing seems to make sense, and the ground seemed to have disappeared from beneath my feet along with my social-cultural habitat. When I noticed that I was in a deep depression, I looked for psychotherapy. Nothing seemed to fit anymore. On the one hand, my dream of being a mom came true. My daughter was the most beautiful, healthy, sweet and smart baby, making me proud and blessed every day. On the other hand, the dark vacuum in my head was very frightening.

It had never occurred even remotely to me that a geographic move could have such an impact on a human being, especially for someone like me, who loves adventures, who loves to learn new things, to face challenges; who is versatile, independent, extroverted, and ready to adjust to unpredictable circumstances. What would be the reasons behind all that?

I moved on, trying to fill up the inner emptiness

by listening to and practicing familiar songs, preparing Brazilian dishes, and talking to family and friends in Brazil by phone and internet. Those were moments of indescribable relief, like little flashes of light on a pitch-dark night.

I was fortunate to meet very interesting friends. Like Karen, an American woman of British background, who had lived in South Africa for years due to work, were she met her ex-husband, the father of her baby, who I came to learn had the same name as mine. She was an anthropologist, with deep knowledge of intercultural phenomena and differences; she was independent, very intelligent, adaptable, sympathetic, beautiful, and young. However, as soon as she faced motherhood in another country, living with a foreign husband, she was overwhelmed by deep depression, as I had been, leading her to leave her husband. She moved back to Connecticut, to live close to her family, counting on their emotional support to raise her baby. She understood very well what I was going through. It was something beyond hormonal changes, post-partum depression, logic, and our understanding up to then. Why had she never experienced depression before, after working and traveling many years through several countries, then suddenly starting to feel powerless, disoriented, and unable to adjust? It was exactly how I used to feel as well.

At the age of thirty-three, before I came to the USA, I had a very good life, being professionally stable.

My private practice in psychology had reached a very comfortable status, seeing an average of fifty clients per week. I was frequently invited to give interviews on mental health subjects on radio stations and to write articles for magazines and newspapers. I also used to enjoy an stable and very well- paid position as a professional singer at São Paulo State Symphonic Orchestra. Having many good friends, and a boyfriend, I used to travel often, nationally and internationally, for work and tourism.

Since 1994, I had lived independently, having my own apartment and loving my freedom and autonomy! This independence had been earned with much work and effort through the years, after two college degrees (piano performance and clinical psychology), and it made me very happy and proud. My goals were to continue my professional growth and to enjoy the life I had built. I had saved enough money to buy a bigger house in São Paulo, the metropolis I grew up in and loved. That would be perhaps the house I would grow old in, with family.

Three years before, I had been invited to develop a music therapy program for patients in an innovative Neurological Intensive Care Unit, at Beneficencia Portuguesa Hospital, one of the best hospitals in São Paulo and South America. It was a pioneer project, as the philosophy of that whole unit specialized in neurological patients. It had been created and managed by a medical team composed of one anesthesiologist, one neurologist/neuro-surgeon, one cardiologist/cardio-surgeon, and one primary care/general surgeon. The project grew and gained positive media attention and a good reputation in the health field. The treatment with music therapy, created and coordinated by me, was generating results, thanks to our scientific efforts; I traveled for six hours every other week, to meet with a professor supervisor from the Federal University of Paraná, who specialized in neurological music therapy. Soon it became a scientific research project, and due to the connection of my supervisor to the Department of Music Therapy of New York University, I was referred and accepted to a master's program in Music Therapy at NYU.

It seemed, on the one hand, an interesting opportunity to expand our knowledge in the field of music therapy and to solidify this project. On the other hand, it seemed a huge risk to lose the professional stability, conquered through years. Moving for two or three years could destabilize a clientele which afterwards would take years to rebuild, along with losing the job at the orchestra. All in all, it would represent a loss of financial freedom and overall stability. Moving from my apartment to work for a master's in the USA, where the cost of education is notoriously high--everything seemed more losses than gains. My thirst for knowledge and professional growth also made me see the opportunity as very seductive. In reality, the risks triggered fear in me, and a great desire to decline the offer--to turn the page and to invest in new paths of professional development in Brazil, where I could stay working and maintain my happy life.

In the mean time, before reaching a decision, I continued working on my three jobs and going on with my normal routines. My life could not be more active and interesting (at least, that was what I used to think). The question was sent to the universe, asking for signs. At times, I was inclined to decline the master's; on other occasions the circumstances made me think that missing it would be a bad idea. My uncertainty about my living situation in the USA constituted a very worrisome issue, making me hesitant. I had no close friends or family around New York City and the possibility of having complete strangers as roommates was unattractive. On the flip side, the facilities and opened doors in regard to the paperwork, all the bureaucracy I had to deal going through the application process, preparing, gathering and officially translating documents, recording auditions and interviews, and how easily all communication with the NYU team was going, were undeniably impressive! I had previously tried to apply for other schools in Europe and everything was much more difficult. So, I valued and appreciated all that ease. Neverthless, my fears regarding the housing situation were reaching their maximum. After working so hard to have my own apartment, and building a comfortable independent life, throwing everything away seemed too crazy and I was about to forget about all that nonsense.

One night, upon my return from work, I received a call from a friend, saying that she had contacted two of her close friends who lived in the USA around NYC. They both had confirmed they had space to have me at their houses as a roommate. My first reaction was: "WHAT?!" But I kept to myself. I could not pronounce a single word, besides "Ummmmm." I was in complete shock! Even though I had mentioned I was in the process of considering a master's program at NYU, I did not recall mentioning any further details, the housing issues, or anything of the sort. Why was this friend, who was not even that close to me, so invested in helping me? Yes, we have spent many weekends together that year, as she, her husband and her two kids used to come and visit my boyfriend's house in São Jose dos Campos, São Paulo State. I had the privilege to perform some concerts there, accompanied by her son's fabulous piano playing, despite his very young age. Due to the financial hardship of that family, my then boyfriend had gifted their son with some formal clothing, as he needed to perform in concerts and events. But none of this seemed proportional to the help she was offering me in regard to the housing situation in NYC. It seemed nothing but providential. The Universe was coordinating things, creating favorable circumstances and giving me clear signs. I thanked her immensely, taking notes of her friends' phone numbers, and followed her advice to call and to check the details directly with them.

I called them the next day. Both were very receptive and friendly. The one who lived in NYC had an small apartment in Manhattan and was already sharing it with three other people. I would be the fifth resident. The convenience of living in Manhattan, very close to the university I would attend, was the biggest advantage. The other, although living much more remotely, in the state of Connecticut, lived in a much more spacious town house, with three bedrooms, and he only lived with two other people. I would have my own room. Then, after meeting new colleagues, I could eventually find a third alternative closer to the school. The pivotal factor in my decision was my intuition. Not knowing either of them in person, for some reason the housing in Connecticut, although much farther, seemed much more attractive to me. As I have long ago learned to trust my sixth sense, I made my decision. After some other conversations with both of them, my trip to the USA started to become tangible and plausible.

The documents and paperwork for the application, selling some of my belongings to generate extra cash for me to take with me, the move, renting my apartment in São Paulo to provide an income source for me during the time in America, the official sponsorship offered by my brother and father as part of the requirement of being an international student in the USA— everything was going smoothly and easily. Slowly I was getting accustomed to the idea of moving forward with this adventure, boosting up my strengths to deal with the financial losses that this would imply.

Among troubles and conflicts with the boyfriend, wonderful English teachers, meeting American friends who moved to São Paulo, sharing their stories and realities of their homeland, the idea of leaving and studying in the USA for two years started to feel closer to reality, along with a peaceful sensation that everything was going to be okay. American music on the radio gained a new meaning, as if that was becoming more and more part of my life each day.

Moving forward and following up with my then current professional obligations before my trip, I went. At the Campos do Jordão Winter Festival of Music, we performed *La Traviata*. The immense theater was packed, despite the freezing winter nights in that mountain city of São Paulo state. All the glamour of the classical music backstage, interviews with radio and TV journalists, cameras, and nationwide live broadcasting, made me feel fulfilled. Many professional musicians would do anything to be in my place, participating in top performances, working with the elite of the professional classical music world of Brazil, South America, and the world. What a privilege!

Saying goodbye to the clients in my practice, whom I had always greatly enjoyed working with, broke my heart--from CEOs and executives to college students, professionals, children and families, each one with his/her own idiosyncrasies, personality, and fascinating saga. Fortunately, they were all well taken care of, with appointments scheduled with their future therapists, referred by me. My secretaries and colleagues, with whom I shared the big and modern office building where we use to practice for years, were part of that very pleasant work environment. Countless interesting and entertaining conversations, between clients, numerous parties, social gatherings and happy hours after work, were shared for years! The good luck card they prepared and signed was full of personal notes and sweet words from each one of them; it is still kept by me with affection to this day.

At the hospital, even though departures were a constant theme there, this time it was different. I was the one leaving, not the discharged patients. The plans upon my return were exciting.

We organized a goodbye party in a pub called "Brain"—nothing could have been more appropriate. We had fun already during the invitation! The large area reserved for our party could not fit all the friends who joined us there, that cold, rainy Friday night! Among great chats, much laughter, dancing, karaoke singing, delicious cocktails and appetizers, the night flew by.

The day of departure arrived. Still very excited by the festivities from the different groups of friends the previous week, I was feeling optimistic and calm. Exchanging jokes and chating with the great group of friends and family who accompanied me to the Cumbica International airport in São Paulo, the hours at that winter August night went by fast. Carrying only two large suitcases with clothing and shoes to spend the two years of the master's program at NYU, I departed onboard that overnight flight to the USA. The trip was calm and without incident; even then, an airplane seat is not what we associate with a good and comfortable night of sleep.

The summer heat was clearly noticeable upon arrival in New York. My friends from Connecticut were waiting for me in the airport and helped me with the luggages. In the car, after the initial introductions and small talk, they warned me that we would drop my luggage at home and go straight to a picnic party. That news penetrated my ears with painful notes. "You must be kidding me!" I said.

"No, we are not.", they replied with laughter. "You have to come with us. You will enjoy it.", they said.

Even though I love a good social gathering, all I wanted at that moment was to collapse somewhere and take a really long nap, after that long flight. However, I could not be anti-social with those nice new friends, who traveled so far just to pick me up at the airport.

Despite the physical distress, feeling foggy after some stressful and busy previous weeks and a sleepless night, the scenery through the car window, seemed surreal. The different vegetation, models of cars, traffic sights, people's biotypes, sounds, smells--everything seemed very interesting and weird at the same time. I was appreciating the different stimuli as an intensive English, history, geography, and sociology class combined.

The friend's house where I was going to live was very cozy, located in an attractive, beautiful, and peculiar neighborhood. Most importantly, the people there were super friendly and sympathetic. My intuition was once more correct! Ah, dear rationalists and skeptical readers, who still have not discovered the value of your intuition, you don't know what you are missing!

The little party was good, the weather was great and warm, with a wonderful sun shining in the sky, people having fun. I decided to practice my English with some old ladies there, who seemed to be impressed with my verbal skills and courage to come here to pursue a master's degree. As if enchanted, one of them said, "I need to introduce you my grandson!" And that casual summer party led me to meet the man who became my husband and father of my daughter.

The food? Well, the first shock! It was a hamburger and hotdog barbecue, with sugary baked beans. The green salad saved the day! "Those Americans don't know what a real barbecue is!" That was the theme of our conversation, among laughs and jokes in the way home.

The next day, already with the neurons back into normality after a good night of sleep, was fun, with visits from other Brazilian friends from New Jersey. They were happy to enjoy my juicy lasagna, Brazilian style, made with ham, bolognese sauce, four cheeses, and white sauce on the top. The following week proceeded with walks through the neighborhood and trips to Manhattan and NYU. There were different routines and procedures at the different departments at school, exchange of documents, signatures, class registration, opening a student email account, orientation meetings with guidance counselors, professors and directors--all part of the regular process of preparing for classes in a couple of weeks.

I fell in love with New York City! Although I had never been there before, I felt completely at home. Its energy, gigantic proportions, and metropolitan rhythm had a lot in common with my home town, São Paulo. In spite of the enthusiasm of being involved in something positive, improving my career, experiencing a new culture, making new friends and feeling very good with all that, at the end of every day I was overcome by an annoying headache. It was the first time I was exposed to a total immersion on a foreign language, 24/7. It is one thing to practice a language in your culture of origin or to travel as a tourist as I have done in Europe before. It is completely different to be immersed in a foreign language all day in everything you do, hear, and say, without a break. It is indescribably exhausting to maintain the best connection with people and reality (which requires a lot of language and communication) under those circumstances.

The commute by train back home, late at night, now seems surreal to me. At that time, however, although stressful, it was pleasant. I empathized with the frenetic lifestyle of the passengers, most of them professionals and workers with jobs in NYC and residing in Connecticut. At times I also felt disgusted to see them eating their "dinners" on those filthy old trains, without washing their hands, placing their cups of coffee or soda, and even containers of their baby's food on the floor impregnated with dirt, while placing their suitcases and belongings on the overhead shelves and getting settled at their seats. Then, they took their "dinner" and enjoyed it as if at home. I wondered how these people didn't get food poisoning and diseases every day. Later, I came to learn through articles and statistics from the American Department of Public Health, that they actually do. According to the American National Institute of Allergies and Infectious Diseases, as well as studies published by the director of Clinical Microbiology of the New York University, Dr. Philip Tierno, more then 80% of the infectious diseases in America are contracted through lack of hand hygiene. A scary 50% of Americans do not wash their hands after using the bathroom and most of the other 50% who wash, do it inefficiently. If they found on gymnastic bars an alarming concentration of residue of feces, along with micro- organisms found in genitals, respiratory flora, salmonella, and hepatitis A and B, what would be found on those quintessentially dirty floors, which besides carrying thousands of people on a daily basis for centuries, are also shelters for rats and other disease-carrying animals? That is very visible. While waiting for the trains everybody can see the rats, pigeons, and cockroaches running through the stations and the trains.

2

NYU

The classes started! Nothing mattered more to me at this moment. This was actually the only reason why I decided to face so many changes and losses. Fortunately, my academic experience at New York University did not disappoint me. Wonderful teachers, each with their own style, were all very attentive and patient, with solid academic knowledge and excellent didactics. Although I had recently arrived from Brazil, and was dealing with cultural adversities, adjustments and idiomatic challenges, especially in the fast rhythm of Manhattan, I still felt at home. I needed to expend extraordinary energy in the classroom to keep up with the teacher's and other students' comments, but my academic performance was surprisingly satisfactory. My mind sent me back in time, as if I were still studying for my first bachelor's degree at Pontific Catholic University of São Paulo. I was rediscovering the pleasure of exchanging scientific knowledge and critical thinking. Nothing can be compared to the exposure of intellectually challenging situations, in an environment with high standards, which demands your very best—an environment fertile to intellectual, professional, and social growth. I had the sensation of utilizing my time and resources well, doing something substantial that made sense, that was worth it. That was to me a great source of emotional, physical, and spiritual well-being. It generated energy and motivation in me.

Spending the day in NYC was an adventure. Departing by train from Connecticut toward Manhattan, I spent long enough traveling to keep up with school reading and projects. There was still time to enjoy the culture, to observe the different individuals who shared the trip with me each day, and to admire the landscape through the train windows. As mentioned before, many, like myself, resided in Connecticut and worked or studied in NYC or surrounding towns. With New York City being overpopulated, but having the largest concentration of jobs of the whole tri-state region, it supports one of the highest housing and living costs. Its real estate market is extremely competitive and much more pricey than all the surrounding area. Even in other states, the closer the property is to Manhattan, the higher is the cost of real estate. With the amount you spend to buy a spacious family home with pleasant finishes and a nice yard in Connecticut, for example, you can only acquire an small studio in Manhattan, the best neighborhood in NYC. If you are lucky, you can find an apartment in Queens, in a dirty, ugly, and unsafe neighborhood, equivalent to some ghettos in South America. That is, by the way, a recurrent situation throughout the northeast of the USA, the most developed area of the country. For that reason, it bothers me deeply hearing pejorative comments about the poverty and hunger in Brazil and South America. Hunger, poverty, and misery are as present here, throughout the underdeveloped neighborhoods of the USA, as they are in South America. And those problems do not affect exclusively the illegal immigrants. The native-born American citizen, even the non-immigrant descendants for more than two generations, who come from a lower-class family, rarely have a chance to raise from poverty. The levels of violence, segregation, and social alienation among individuals of lower classes, have an oppressive and deflating effect on their lives, personality, and self-esteem.

The classes continued, my English kept improving, I kept meeting new friends and widening my horizons. The building where we had most of the classes was shared with the music performance department. I just loved to peek through the windows and half-open doors to watch some instrumental and singing classes. New York, being one of the most important performance and economic capitals of the world, offers some the best performing arts schools in the world. I felt alive, and all those challenges reassured me that my sacrifices were worth it.

So far, the cultural shock was not being experienced negatively. Inserted into a very stimulating academic environment, I widened my intellectual and personal background, feeling respected intellectually, as a person and as a professional, gaining respect from the teachers through good academic performance and excellent grades. In this regard, there was nothing different from my reality in Brazil. With my identity preserved, no destructive impact was experienced.

I concluded the academic year with my GPA at 4.0! I was very happy upon receipt of the school records! Not so bad for a third-world student! I experienced my success as a collective victory, a dignifying representation of my country, expressing who we really are and are capable of--very different from the usual stereotypes, assuming we are all illiterate savages from jungles or favelas. To the contrary, my performance was the result of extensive academic and scientific experiences back in my own country, prior to coming here. Due to the excellent levels of college education I received there, I didn't find any difficulty presenting the same excellence in a foreign country, despite the language barrier.

3

MOTHERHOOD

I decided to stop temporarily my studies at the university and take time to enjoy my pregnancy and to take care of my baby. Initially, everything went well. I was going to be a mom, which, despite not being planned at that time, brought me immense joy. The pregnancy developed normally and I gave birth to the healthiest and most beautiful baby in the world! I cultivated new friendships with other new moms. We used to meet every morning to walks with our babies, followed by some chat and tea at a café in downtown New Haven. We attended post-partum gym classes. They were pure happiness shots! I had never before experienced the mood-enhancing power of a good cardio workout. I used to leave the classes full of energy, as if I could fly and conquer the world! Unfortunately, they lasted only a few weeks at that gym and there were no other specialized classes for post-partum women in the small town of New Haven.

The sleepless nights, breastfeeding every two hours, a life lacking stimulation in the inert towns of Connecticut, the lack of intellectual stimuli of the life there, the constant stress dealing with my mother-in-law (which could very well be another book!), missing the stimulating bits of São Paulo and New York, along with the post-partum hormone changes...little by little it all started to consume me. I looked for therapy and it was going well, until one day I was taken by a sudden desperation, a terrifying sensation of losing myself, an intense and debilitating anxiety. That summer weekend, I requested to be taken to the hospital. After the initial intake, they did not want to admit me to a psychiatric unit, but I requested to stay in the general hospital infirmary. Since I had an outpatient therapist and was breastfeeding, they did not want to give me any medication.

Those were the worst days of my life. The transition from the breast milk to the formula bottle was not going well, thanks to the insistence of the pediatrician on call, to give the baby only soy-based baby formula, that horrendous thing, which my daughter, with good reason, did not take. Regardless of my deplorable mental status, without any sleep for weeks, light-headed and dizzy, by the second day, I managed to stamp my foot and say that I was going to give her the animal-based baby formula, defying that pediatrician. I went home, prepared the new formula, and my daughter took the whole bottle without stopping, with those little blue eyes looking directly into mine, which started pouring tears of happiness. She had no allergic reaction whatsoever, contrary to what that insensitive pediatrician was categorically affirming. Once again the maternal instincts overwrote the statistical medical knowledge. As a psychologist I must say that many medical doctors NEED to develop their sensitivity and the respect for their patient's opinions and input. To learn to work WITH their patients, leaving aside, for once, their omnipotent and absolutely pretentious postures of "gods" and owners of the truth, an attitude still peculiar to this professional class. No one knows their own bodies better than the patients themselves, and the mothers know the most about their babies. Regardless of the scientific knowledge and medical training they may carry, the intuition, the intrinsic and practical knowledge of the individuals, about themselves, and the mothers about their babies, are essential for more precise diagnosis and treatment. The role of the health professionals is to CONTRIBUTE with their scientific knowledge and experience, adding it as a tool to promote health and well-being to their patients, who are the ones who pursue ALL the rights and power over their own lives and health. As a health professional myself, working with multi-disciplinary teams for over twenty-five years in different settings, I can affirm that medicine is categorically not a precise science. Much knowledge indeed exists and has been accumulated to this day. However, there is always subjectivity, from both the patients and the professionals involved in the processes of disease, diagnostics, treatment, and cure. And this absolutely cannot be ignored in the doctor-patient relationship.

Monday arrived, after that eternal weekend. First thing in the morning, after the hygiene and morning care of the baby, I went to visit my therapist, who was also a nurse. I requested to be prescribed an anti-depressant, after I told her what happened throughout the weekend. Since the transition to the bottle was already completed successfully, that was what she did.

The side effects in the first weeks were terrible. I decreased the dosage in half and put up with it for another week. Slowly the nausea, anxiety, and lack of appetite started to fade and I finally started to breathe normally. The social isolation was still a difficult and destabilizing factor to deal with. Although I had that small group of moms, a few other Brazilian friends, and some graduate students of Yale University, having passed at the Yale choir audition, having received an invitation to play piano, organ, and sing at a Congregational church nearby, I still didn't feel the same level of happiness I used to feel in NYC and São Paulo.

When my daughter was three months old, we had the consecration ceremony at the church. My parents came, along with two of my brothers. It felt like a dream! I am certain that they had no idea how important that visit was to me. It was as if I had been submerged under deep and dark waters, and suddenly was brought up to the surface. After the ceremony and the reception, my brothers went back to NYC on their tourist agenda. My parents stayed with us the whole time, as I would do and have done for them. They came to visit me, giving me the support I so much needed. As they had done many times throughout my life, they always put their children's needs above their own. There will never be enough words to express my gratitude to them for their altruism and the emotional support they gave me.

Those weeks were magical and wonderfully revitalizing to me. Seeing them enjoying and having fun with their new granddaughter, keeping me company, was something extremely and indescribably positive. We used to go out for walks, and drove to grocery stores and places close by, as I had an international driver's license. We went to New York by train one day. My parents were elderly already. My father was very debilitated after a cancer treatment, and could not walk for long. The three of us (me and my parents) still managed to enjoy the trip very much, visiting Grand Central Station, Central Park, and the Statue of Liberty. I felt somehow worried and guilty for exposing them to such stress, but then I felt relieved when my dad said with satisfaction, "I never imagined I would still be able to visit New York at this stage of my life."

The last days were somehow frustrating since I had to study for the written exam for my Connecticut driver's license. I barely had time to go out with them anymore, and once more their emotional support was extremely touching. At last, I took the test, passed, and when I got my license it was the day they had to go back to São Paulo. The goodbyes were hard, but I considered myself very privileged to have such wonderful parents, and great role models. With them I have learned the meaning of altruism and unconditional love, and the value and power of a genuinely good heart, capable of placing the needs of others before their own. This certainly gave me the foundation and the excellent example to be utilized in my own motherhood.

I proceeded to my normal routine. On the one hand, I felt privileged to be able to dedicate myself to the care of my baby, to see her growing healthy, secure, and happy. At the same time, after a couple of years 100% immersed in the domestic and maternal world, the daily routines became boring.

My daughter was two years old now. It seemed it was time to resume my studies and career. Although I was not feeling so happy with my life in America, the idea of returning to Brazil to live, with those new circumstances, appeared to be as risky as a staying. My husband, with almost no Portuguese skills and only one BA degree in creative writing, didn't have the tools to compete and succeed in the job market in São Paulo, full of highly qualified professionals. Most importantly, despite his affinity for and admiration of the Brazilian culture and lifestyle along with his willingness to follow me to Brazil if I wanted to move there, his nature, with extreme difficulties adjusting to change, told me that his adaptation would be more difficult than mine. After three years in America, I also would be restarting over careerwise in Brazil, building a new clientele, no longer having my position at the orchestra. Having a toddler, without financial stability, having to work full time, would make the re-adjustment even more stressful or even unbearable. At this point, my perspective on life were very different from before my departure. After all, living in a foreign country and experiencing immersion into another culture causes substantial and permanent changes in one's identity, making one feel foreign in their own culture of origin after a while. It was not any different in my case.

4

BACK TO BRAZIL

Our first visit to my family in Brazil, after moving to the USA, was amazing. My daughter was nine months old. The preparation, the trip, and the arrival were all exciting experiences. My daughter did not cry at all in the plane, through turbulence, and the brutal changes in altitude and air pressures during that nine-hour flight. I have never seen such a sweet and mature little baby! Her intense discomfort, at different moments, was noticeable. Even for us adults, our ears were hurting and we were dizzy at times. It was impossible that such delicate baby's body was not suffering with all that. But she simply sucked the bottle or her little thumb, having those little blue eyes wide open and glued to mine, with a very serious, almost frozen facial expression, keeping quiet like an angel.

The arrival was almost comical. We brought so many suitcases with gifts to everyone, that it seemed we must be moving there. Already at the airport, I felt a tremendous and incredible emotion, stepping again on familiar homeland. Everyone in the streets was perceived as brothers and sisters, and I was taken by a warm desire to hug each one of them, as a veteran back from war. After the experiences of those two years, the return represented rescuing myself. The energy, the sounds, the smells, the faces, the landscape, the language--everything made me feel grounded and back from a bad dream.

We got all suitcases. There was a huge Ferreira committee awaiting for us by the gates. The warm hugs and kisses, soaked with happy tears, the excitement which made our hearts race, were like oasis water on the desert. I could hug and kiss my family and friends as much as I wanted, without being judged or feeling inappropriate, as I would in America. The physical contact all the time, typical of the Brazilian culture and communication, was deeply missed. We could talk and laugh out loud, as this was the norm among family and friends--the freedom of expression in its fullness! Those who never experienced moving from a liberal and warm culture to a strict and cold one cannot understand the extent of the oppression that this represents in one's soul. Communication is something much deeper and wider then the expression and understanding of words, as we have explored in the Chapter "The Immigrant and Communication."

Daddy waited for us by the door with open arms, and a big smile that could not be contained. Mommy and her maid had prepared a delicious and abundant meal. It's a typical Brazilian habit to receive visitors with abundant meals, with the visitors' favorite dishes. I could never have imagine that in cultures that call themselves luxurious, sharing a meal would be something so restricted and minimalistic. In America, people eat too much, have a poor-quality diet and share very little. The parties and social gatherings have time strictly restrained and last a very short time. In visits to friends, the absence of culinary compliments and gastronomic courtesies reflect the coldness of their winter in the northeast. Even a glass of water, or a little cup of coffee or tea are not part of their welcome. At this point, after a long and spooky winter of emotional snowstorms, everything from home would be my favorite dish.

Coming from a large family, our home was always full of people and happiness. As the youngest child, my older siblings and me had a huge age gap. My second oldest sister already had grandkids and my grandnieces, three and four years old at that time, were delighted to play with the new American mascot cousin.

It was a typical weekend day. We passed the hours eating, chatting, and laughing by the dining table. We alternated preparing meals and snacks for the kids, who were playing or napping in the other room. Sometimes we would go to the back yard to play with the dog. The next day, most of them came back for more chatting and to make plans for the rest of the week.

We left New York in a bitter winter that year, with temperatures bellow zero Celsius and arrived to that fantastic summer. We had fun comparing the pictures, from snowmen and eskimo's accoutrements, to swim-suits by the pool during those delicious sunny days.

Through visits to parks, zoos, malls, and social gatherings with friends and family, the three weeks went by very fast. Those were incredibly happy days!

5

RETURNING TO THE STATES

The flight was full and the trip seemed much longer. Already by the time we landed, the gray skies and the monotonous white landscape triggered great sadness, as if we were coming back from a good dream to a harsh reality. I felt the effects of the weather immediately, like an electrical switch, shutting down the light. No longer taken by the enthusiasm of embracing new academic adventures or the summer that welcomed me the first time, I was feeling blue. I still had several months ahead of a frozen, grumpy, and insolent winter, waiting for me. The dull and dreary scenery, the nude vegetation, the people with muscles, faces, and hearts hardened to cope with the bitter snowstorms, pouring down from the sky in buckets.

It made me recall the resilience of the first European pioneers in the colonial times, arriving here to land and climate even more difficult than what they had come from, with no health resources, infrastructure, electricity, or sewer system. They had only their tenacity, courage, and thirst to build a new life. Without running water, they could not shower. Deprived of bathing for months of physical labor, living pilled up in small wooden hovels, with dirt floors, they accumulated dirt and sweat on their smelly bodies. At least nowadays we could count on warm showers every day, electricity, and central heating. We were able to cook and to store food in fridges, we had machines to wash and to dry clothes, entertainment through TV, radio and internet--we could hibernate more comfortably.

Then I was back to my daily routine in the land of Uncle Sam. Among music therapy courses at NYU, working as a pianist and organist in churches in Connecticut and NY, voice classes with students, concerts, recitals, and my maternal and domestic obligations, the days were passing.

6

FURTHERING MY STUDIES AND CAREER

After a long process of application and auditions, I received a letter of acceptance to another master's program, this time in opera at Boston Conservatory, one of the most renowed performing arts schools in the USA. The biggest difficulty was separating from my daughter. After caring for that little innocent and vulnerable angel twenty-four hours a day for three consecutive years, leaving her in daycare was heartbreaking. The hardship was mutual, making it even harder for me. The subway train commutes from home to the daycare, then to school and back daily, required determination and endurance. The commitment succeeded through warm, rainy, frozen, and snowy days. We constantly had short sleepless nights due to colds, asthma, coughs and fever. Attending school, my daughter now started to develop respiratory illnesses often. By the second year, I had to reach every bit of inner energy to attend classes, rehearsals until late at night, concerts, and to study. On the weekends I also had a part-time job as a church music director and another during the week as a bilingual domestic violence advocate and counselor. But I was happy and grateful for the opportunities to be back to school and to work.

The competitive job market in the opera world, especially for sopranos, and my dislike of teaching music, made it difficult to pay the bills only with music. Some opportunities came to me to work in opera companies in Europe (Wales-United Kingdom, Montpelier-France) but with family, the move would be difficult. A large percentage of professional opera singers, who are able to maintain a successful career as performers, are single, and only 13% of the married ones have kids. The whole glamour seen on the stages with the big stars carries the high cost of a solitary personal life without roots. The ones who refuse to engage into a nomadic lifestyle, end up needing to subject themself to parallel jobs. The musicians without further qualifications in other fields, many times feel forced to subject themselves to unqualified and less dignifying jobs, like waitressing, retail, etc., in order have their financial needs met.

In my case the opportunities in psychology were numerous. I continued working with music, but also needed to complement my budget through jobs in the health field. Without a license in America, the positions

I could be hired were at non-profit organizations and the pay was minimal. I decided to go toward a fifth college degree, a master's in psychology to ensure I had the requirements for a license and better salary. Although much less exciting, the course went by fast and without problems. The teachers who really made a positive impact, adding knowledge, were the lecturers. Some of them I keep in contact with to this day.

Notwithstanding the difficulties of the life as an immigrant, the adjustments, the restructuring of life in every aspect, (personal, psychological, financial, and professional), I knew the advantages of having multi-language and multi-cultural skills were extremely useful and wanted in the mental health field.

My horizons were widened through my own experiences. I had the opportunity to acquire maturity, knowledge, new personal skills, and a deeper view of myself, others, life, and the world. This led me to a better understanding and development of new techniques, significantly more effective, to treat many disorders, not only pertaining to immigrants' lives, but to everyone. Through a personal quest for answers and solutions for crises and disorders triggered by the acculturation process, today I am able to treat cases of trauma, depression, anxiety, obsessive-compulsive disorders, phobias, eating disorders, marital and family issues, and provide training in parenting skills with much more efficacy, thanks to my experiences as an immigrant.

Personal transformations, especially from experiences of loss, can and need to be transformed into knowledge to benefit the collective, to make it worth it. If the alchemy does not produce gold, the burning of the fire will be useless.

7

THE MIGRATING BUTTERFLIES

The universe conspires in our favor, leading us to accomplishments, the fulfillment of our dreams, toward personal growth, when we do our part and we can see the signs. Today, after I listened to one of the most inspiring songs ("What a Wonderful World" by Louis Armstrong) , I participated in a reflection about the law of attraction and synchronicity. Nothing happens by accident; there is a purpose to everything in life and in nature.

One of the most common species of butterfly in the northern hemisphere is the monarch. Their lives are fascinating, if we learn a little more in depth. During their migration process, they leave from north to the south, starting their journey mid- August, from Canada and the USA, flying toward the south, mating along the way. Their eggs go through their own processes, from caterpillars to new butterflies until the third or fourth generation arrives in Mexico at the end of October to the beginning of November. That is exactly the time when the Mexicans celebrate the "Day of the Dead."

The Mexicans welcome the arrival of the butterflies, as the spirits of their ancestors who are joining them to the festivities in their honor. Greek mythology, coincidentally, also describes butterflies as the souls of their deceased loved ones. Considering the apparent fragility of those insects, vulnerable to all climate conditions, having their lives in risk by storms, rains, intense temperatures, direction and intensity of the winds, predators, nectar availability during the trip, the exact time they need to spend between mating, eating, and flying, always fighting against all sorts of adversities, it seems a miracle that this phenomenon occurs repeatedly every year. They migrate south at the end of summer, returning to the north at the end of winter, at the beginning of spring (February and March).

There is no doubt that much can be learned from nature. The butterflies teach us that, regardless of our adversities, the secrets of surviving the migration process are:

1- Keep focused on your final goal, your destiny as an individual. Every immigrant, one way or another, was led by life circumstances, to leave their native habitat toward foreign lands, reaching for their survival, a better life or to open their horizons, which unconsciously leads to the survival of our species. Regardless of the individual reasons why one searches for immigration, it is always associated with an ingrained need of the soul that needs to be fulfilled.

2- The synchronicity of the climate, folkloric, cultural, and biological phenomena involved in the monarchs' migration process can be correlated to the understanding of our life circumstances. When we observe those details closely, perfectly connecting and interrelating all those factors, year after year, it's foolish to think of them as coincidences, or random chance, failing to see the correlation of each aspect and detail, as part of a large thread called the ecosystem, which includes us, the human race. Despite our free will and ability to function beyond our animal instincts, we still belong to nature. We are part of this immense universe, and have certainly been influenced by it in more ways than we think. In the same way the butterflies sense the direction they should follow, even when their moms are far gone by the time they become a butterfly, we are also capable of feeling the energy in the air, as Early Man did, going toward foreign lands in search of evolution. The laws of attraction and synchronicity are phenomena on the same order of those synchronized factors that happen in nature: pure physics, which determines the development of facts in one's individual life, as well as our collective destiny. Physiologically, psychologically, sociologically, politically, interpersonally, individually, collectively speaking, everything is subject to energetic forces, both created and influenced by each other, the same way that the elements of nature are attached, interdependent, and influenced by each other, at this energetic ecosystem, in ways that transcend our sight.

3- The monarchs teach us the keys to the adjustment through the immigration process. They simply utilize the best of each moment and location. They don't get attached to previous places or seasons, but stay focused on the present and their future.

8

DEVELOPING COPING
MECHANISMS

The summer is almost over. It seems that each year, time goes faster! Although I enjoyed the wonderful warm weather I so much love, this last summer was not experienced as empowering as the previous ones. The freedom I feel, being able to come and go easily any time, by sunrise or sunset, the daily walks and jogs outside, before and after work, without the freezing winds or the slippery streets, may not seem so meaningful. Nevertheless, those who live this reality year after year know how restraining and debilitating the harsh winters can be to our plans and daily routines.

Fortunately, they no longer determine my mood as they once did. I remember when I opened the second branch of my office in Massachusetts, years ago. It was in the middle of the winter and it was one of the best times of my life in America. I had found this very cozy office to rent. My clientele multiplied so rapidly that year, that it all seemed like a dream. It was a very remarkable and enlightening year in regard to understanding the effect of the weather on one's mood. The lack of sunlight in the short winter days has, in fact, a neurophysiological effect. The decreased production of serotonin in the brain causes individuals to feel blue or even depressed. The famous seasonal depression debilitates many during the winter, even those who where born and raised in cold climate locations. However, there are other factors we can explore and develop in order to cope. That year the winter was experienced with much joy. The new perspectives triggered excitement, and I have experienced the same thing this year, writing this book. The short and cold days, the snowstorms, depriving me of many outside activities, represent an awesome opportunity to develop new projects, especially those that require silence and can be done indoors.

It became very evident throughout the years in my practice, a significant increase of depression cases during the winter, with a decline of people's mental status and functionality, due to the effect of the shorter daylight on people's circadian cycles this time of the year. Statistical data support the same conclusion. Physical exercise is fundamental to maintenance of mental health, especially in cold weather places. Developing compensatory coping mechanisms are also necessary to avoid decompensation. There are multiple coping mechanisms that can be individually developed through a therapeutic process. Ultimately, finding meaning in our lives in any circumstance is crucial to reach or maintain a healthy mental status.

Without a doubt, the adjustment to the weather, associated with other factors, such as diet, freedom of expression, freedom of coming and going, circadian cycle, etc., represent some of the biggest challenges for most immigrants, even for those who migrate from one region of the country to another. For the immigrant, it also triggers a dissonance between the native and the new environment.

There was a study done by a Canadian professor published by Pearce, which observed the musical vibration of the different geographic locations and their influences in the individuals. He observed that the environment carries a natural vibration, which was translated into musicality and rhythms, and is perceived unconciously by the individuals. He goes further, mentioning the fact that each individual also carries his/her own indiosyncratic neuro-psychic-physiological harmonic frequencies. Therefore, it's easy to assume a correlation between the individual and his/her environment, which imposes an strong impression into one's organism. If this relation is harmonious, it will promote health and well-being, at physical and mental levels. If it is not, it can cause a deep discomfort or even disease. Regardless of the individual's plasticity and adaptability, sometimes the cost of this adaptation can be too high and generate illness.

Such adaptation to the environment, besides being painful at times, can also trigger changes in conduct, behavior, ways of thinking and feeling, at deeper, visceral levels not experienced consciously. The vibrational influences, through sounds and other kinds of energy, perceived only at the visceral and unconscious levels, trigger organic reactions and automatic responses toward adaptation. The multiple particularities of this process can generate illnesses and chronic imbalances, or can trigger positive changes, benefits, and enrichment of one's internal resources, valuable advantages, which would not be developed without the exposure to the dissonant circumstance. Somehow, that is the baseline of evolution. Successful positive changes and adaptations are acquired by individuals, groups, and species, from adverse, potentially life-threathning environmental circumstances. Those adaptative changes become ultimately ingrained in DNA and passed to future generations. We are focusing here on the migration process; however, environmental changes can also happen, spontaneously, although those are less frequent.

It is known that we are somehow determined by our genetic tendencies, along with our social-political-economic reality (such as access to good health care, and healthfulness of our physical and psychological environment) along with our choices toward a healthy life. However, this study opens our eyes to the numerous environmental factors that play important roles for our body, mind, and overall being, still underrated and unknown both to science and to common sense. One way or the other, it gives us a better idea about the dimension of the impact that a new geographic environment has on the individual, positively or negatively.

Therefore, the immigration adjustment process is much deeper than has been previously understood. It involves physical-energetic-vibrational phenomena of the environment, interacting and interfering directly to the physical-energetic-vibrational phenomena of the individual. This is contrary to what is understood in the common sense, that simple acquisition of foreign language skills, a superficial learning of foreign habits, culinary practices, laws, and geography, would be sufficient to guarantee a good adjustment. Such visceral and vibrational impacts of a new environment on the immigrant, are far from being fully understood, particularly by those who have never experienced a cultural shock. Those new scientific perspectives, however, help us to better understand the deep emotional crisis as well as the development of medical and psychiatric disorders, common after a migratory transition, even in cases related to an improvement of socio-economic levels and/or when there was desire for and planning toward the move.

9

UNDER THE RADAR

It's my dad's birthday. He would be ninety-four years old. His memories keep me company throughout the day. A mixture of longing and gratitude for his presence and help from the ethereal world takes my heart.

Nevertheless, I was unfairly stopped by a traffic police with a mobile radar. The more we observe the facts and our rights, the more we notice the arbitrary nature of "law" enforcement. Before, I used to think those problems only happened in Latin America, countries built as exploitation colonies by Portugal and Spain. There, in colonial times, the concept of respect for the citizen did not exist, as citizens were seen, by definition, as mere instruments to generate wealth. However, this is very prevalent in North America as well, especially the USA, only it is disguised through corporativism and institutionalization.

I observed beforehand the intensity of the traffic, passing through that narrow and busy street in

Cambridge. While I waited for the policeman to arrive at my car after stopping, I video recorded all this with my cell phone.

The young officer arrived reticent, with a shy attitude, unwilling to meet my eyes. I looked at him planted by my left window. After a couple of seconds, he said "Hi," like a child testing his limits. When I answered and he noticed my accent, his whole posture was transformed. His chest inflated, he opened his legs, planting his feet apart from each other, he moved to look me with full face and lowered the pitch of his voice. "Do you want to know how fast you were driving?" he asked me with an intimidating facial expression. I said, "Yes." He showed me the number 45 (mile/hr.) on a manual beam radar, which he exhibited like a cool new toy. I replied that it was not what my car was showing when he stopped me. I was sure I was not above the speed limit, as he was trying to convince me otherwise, showing me the number again. I noticed also that I was surrounded by other cars on both sides, front and back at very close distances, driving at the same speed, as the traffic was intense when he stopped me. Why I was the only one stopped? How he could be so sure that the speed registered on his manual radar was from my car and not from the others? Was that an inaccurate result?

My initial observation did not change his intention. He looked at me allegedly as an easy target to fulfill his quota and to collect his bonus. I memorized very well the appearance of that machine. I handled him my driver's license and car registration, as requested. While he was back to his vehicle to consult the computers and to issue the potential ticket, I observed his partner, a lady officer appearing to be much older and more experienced, also holding a similar radar and gesturing to the cars to slow down. Nobody else was stopped. I counted at least ten other cars, driving much faster than I was driving and being noticed by both officers, who acted condescendingly. Absolutely nobody else stopped. I registered everything with my cell video camera.

He was coming back this time with wide and assertive steps and an inflated chest, like someone who just killed a lion: "Bad news," he said. "Here is your speeding ticket." He handed it to me, along with my driver's license and car registration. I got the documents, kept them back, and stayed parked there for a while, videotaping the traffic and their actions. The same scenario played out for fifteen more minutes. Cars were speeding, and nobody else was stopped.

Back home, I researched to verify the questions I had in my mind about the validity of that ticket. I checked in public records and on legal sites to research images and descriptions of the different radars. The radar that had targeted me was a manual beam speed gun. According to experts, and published research from physics articles and attorneys, its precision is questionable, as it requires specific conditions to register a precise speed:

a) The operator (in this case, the police officer) needs to focus and hold the beam gun on a central and unchangeable point in the car, keeping the speed gun absolutely static at this specific and initial point. If the beam is moved to another point during the time it needs to register the speed of the car (due to involuntary movement of the hand, shaking, bumpy roads, etc.) the speed gun will register a false reading.

b) Even if the conditions above are fulfilled, the beam of frequency wave or even the laser will capture also the speed of other cars around the initial target, if they are passing close by. It can even capture the velocity of other objects in the environment, such as flying leaves or moving branches of trees, on a windy day.

c) Manual radars (or speed guns) rarely work precisely in traffic, as a significant separation between the cars is essential to correct operation. When more than one object is moving within the wave frequency field of a mobile radar, the captured speed cannot be recognized as precise.

These were exactly the conditions under which I received my ticket. Having scientific data along with recorded evidence to prove the inconsistency of this ticket, I checked the appeal option, sent it to the return address, and went to the hearing with the court clerk and judge.

I observed, then, in retrospect, that similar circumstances were involved in most of my previous tickets--not necessarily involving speeding, but with inconsistent "evidence," which would definitely qualify them for dismissal. Therefore, my civil rights had been violated for years, and with me, thousands of other citizens.

At the audience with the judge, the police officer described the incident at the judge's request. Many important data were described incorrectly, such as the make and model of my car, the type and reliability of the radar he used, the conditions under which the ticket occurred, etc. I presented my questions to the judge when prompted by her, raising the discrepancies on the data the officer presented, the circumstances involved in the situation, including the intense traffic, close proximity with the other cars on that very bumpy road, and how much that would make the only evidence he had to write down the ticket not reliable and inconsistent. In his own description in the court, the police officer explained that the speed is recorded on the speed gun by focusing on a specific point in the car, the license plate, holding there for certain time, and that would be sufficient to ensure a precise result. As I have mentioned, on that bumpy road, in terrible condition after the harsh winter we had that year, it would be absolutely impossible to maintain the gun focused on one point in the car. The car was constantly moving up and down due to the potholes, making this precision absolutely implausible. That alone would be a reason to dismiss the case.

However, I had an accent, so her eyes were rolling throughout my questions and arguments against the reliability of the data. She just ignored everything and ordered me to pay the full amount. Proving that the decision was arbitrary is that on another occasion I had an attorney representing me with the same arguments, and the case was dismissed within a couple of minutes.

To some, all this may sound like victimization or finding excuses to get away with breaking the law. However, any minority citizen can confirm that they have experienced similar circumstances, being placed in unfair situations, due to the different parameters under which Caucasian Americans and all other ethnic groups are judged and treated in America. As mentioned in the introduction, the purpose of this book is not related to personal reasons, to make complaints or to ask for pity from anyone. On the contrary, I consider myself privileged, thanks to the academic background and opportunities I had throughout my life, both here and in Brazil. However, the social issues need to be highlighted, and only those who experience them are able to bring them up to the awareness of society as a whole. This way we can all work toward the necessary changes, which will certainly benefit everyone.

As a psychologist, I witness and listen to incidents of arbitrary law enforcement all the time. Besides listening to my clients' stories, I also observe the inner world of the law enforcement and judicial system, working in partnership with attorneys, helping shared clients in different cases, such as DUI, anger management, family issues, custody of children, divorce, and Immigration cases. The favoritism and arbitrary measures are a constant on the back stage of the legal system. Comments like: "This judge does not like that person or attorney, therefore he/she will favor the opponent," or "The voice and manner of such and such person, irritates me, therefore I am helping his/her opponent." When I face such situations, I put in an extra effort not to fall into the same mistakes, keeping an objective, fair and professional attitude, without being taken by the peer pressure or the corporativism of the team. I base my conclusions, reccomendations, and overall analysis on objective and clinical data alone, leaving subjectivity out of the equation. I feel extremely bad when I see this happening, as people's lives are being deeply affected by those professionals and authorities. That is exactly the foundation of all discrimination, segregation, and injustice.

It is very clear to me that a psychological or medical evaluation, as well as decisions made by law enforcement and legal professionals, cannot be based on subjectivity, personal preferences, or any kind of favoritism. That is what, by the way, we all swear to do when we get our diplomas and licenses in all those fields. Nevertheless, in reality, this does not always occur. Distortions are recurrent and common practices. The lives of the people involved are not taken at all into consideration. What many or even most people fail to realize is that one can feel good doing this, if that makes one feel part of the mainstream or the "dominant/ accepted group"--having the power to decide another's destiny. As long as they feel accepted, belonging to their group and supported by them, they do not think about the consequencies of such arbitrary behavior on people's lives. However, the situation could and can be reversed at any time, and one can never know, when they will be the one in the position of being unfairly judged or treated. Only then, they would feel such arbitrariness as unfair and injust. That is an issue that can happen with any type of person and at any level of life and society, from social groups to family to high schoolers to professional levels. Only in professional contexts is nondiscrimination supposedly enforced, and those subjective, allegedly unethical, and unprofessional attitudes should never take place. The economic, legal, and political systems cannot be managed like high school groups. However, the more we are able to evolve away those behaviors in a personal level, the easier it becomes to assure equality in professional and social realms.

Not doing to others what we don't want others to do to us should always be our standard in life. As in every social change, here or in any part of the world, now and at all times, becoming aware of the issue is essential and the first step toward its solution.

These days, the news is full of information about massacres against African-Americans in the South, mass shootings in black churches and communities in different locations, many by one single white armed man, different in each attack. For centuries, black and minority communities have been victims of injustice, segregation, and violence. The media, however, tends to hide, distort, or dimish those facts. The news being presented now is, according to expert analysis, a political strategy to demoralize even more the current president, an African-American man, regardless of his overwhelming, endless, and articulate efforts to promote social justice and diplomatic negotiations.

Awareness of these problems needs to increase. If not for the movements and initiatives of Martin Luther King Jr., Rosa Parks, Abraham Lincoln, and others, those problems would be even worse today. If not for the feminist movements since the late 19th century in the USA, the United Kingdom, Canada, and the Netherlands, fighting for gender's equality, women still would not have basic civil rights, such as voting, worker's compensation, criminalization of domestic violence and rape, etc. Despite many steps toward social justice and equality, discrimination and injustice still prevail. Laws are not enough to change people's morals, values, and behavior. As we have mentioned, the distortion of facts and unjust outcomes will still occur, using corporativism, institutionalized prejudice, and abuse of power, all used to perpetuate the old segregational values and discrimination now implemented in disguise. The laws evolved somehow, but the social values did not follow the same route at the same pace. If people do not change their inner beliefs, values, and morals, laws will continue to be distorted and utilized solely as a mechanism of oppression of the already oppressed.

As the blacks and women, it is necessary to raise awareness about the discrimination and injustice vastly perpetuated against Latinos, Brazilians, Spanish speakers, and all the other minorities, whether legal or illegal immigrants.

I have focused here predominantly on data from and the reality of the USA, simply due to the fact I am living, experiencing, and working here, gathering personal and clinical information pertaining to this country as a psychotherapist. However, those issues are universal, and are reflexes of the still underdeveloped moral standards of humanity.

I am certain, though, that humanity is capable of evolution, as we can observe through history. From wild, barbarian, and slave-owning civilizations we developed some timid steps toward laws and regulations related to civil and human rights and equality.

Much effort still needs to be made to continue this growth toward a deep and ingrained transformation, through which we all can naturally think and feel respectful toward one another, not for fear of being reprimanded by the law, but simply because that would be our norm, both on personal and collective levels. To evolve toward cooperation instead of competition; love instead of hatred; compassion and peace instead of war; and acceptance, respect, and peaceful coexistence of different people, instead of discrimination and segregation. When we get there, we will realize that we all will be winners. But then we will have a victory free of revenge, karma, or counter-attacks. History repeatedly shows us the result of false victories, conquered through competitive and oppressive means. The Egyptians, the Greeks, the Romans, the British, the Nazis, etc, all conquered through oppression. They rose and fell, as those methods are unsustainable in the long term. Oppression attracts oppression, exploitation and disrespect attract revolt and rebellion, violence creates violence. That is the physical law of cause and effect. The roles are at some point reversed and the powerful become the oppressed, in this endless cyclical tragedy of the human saga.

Our lives will be better when, at last, we can learn this lesson, which we have repeatedly failed to learn, century after century, era after era--when we at last are able to create, inside and outside of ourselves, higher and more enlightened parameters, based on altruism, love, acceptance, respect, and peace among all beings, without exception, not merely through laws, but by naturally living by those higher moral principles, feelings, intentions, and values.

In one metaphorical story, an individual was taken

to hell and to heaven after his death. When he initially arrived in hell, he was surprised to see a large and fine banquet. Confused, he asked his master, "Are you sure this is hell? This fine table, fulfilled with abundant gourmet food, seems more like heaven to me."

The wise master calmly responded, "Wait for the arrival of the other inhabitants, and you will understand."

The rest of the company entered the room with mutual slaps, aggressions, pushes, insults, and kicks, carrying abnormally large forks, made from heavy metal and in inconveniently large proportions to be utilized in that space. In vain they tried to satisfy their hunger with that delicious and well-prepared food. Overwhelmed with anguish and desperation, they all fainted in hunger and from diseases after days of unsuccessfully trying to eat.

The master then took the recently deceased to heaven. Greatly surprised, he commented upon arrival,

"How can we be in heaven if the table in front of us is identical to the one in hell?"

The master, similarly responded, "Wait to see its inhabitants."

The people arrived at the premises, bringing a gentle demeanor and the same oversized, heavy forks in their hands. However, upon arrival at the table, the surprise of the visitor turned into tears of joy by witnessing the gentleness and cordiality in which they behaved, feeding each other with those gigantic utensils, which now were just perfect to reach each other's mouths. This way, they were all equally satisfied, happy, feeling mutually respected, included, and safe. Peace and happiness prevailed amoung them effortlessly, after at last having learned that the only way to solve their problem was to help and care for each other.

Similarly, the moral evolution of humankind is the only way for us to definitely reach social justice and equality. Laws can be established and they are the beginning of this process. However, until we reach an authentic and essential moral growth, starting on the individual level and extending to the collective, the laws will be distorted and disobeyed by many, including the authorities themselves, and arbitrariness will continue to occur. Such distortions, manipulations, and arbitrary interpretations of the law by the authorities, in our present society, are for example represented by the lawlessness and misdeeds of the economic oligarchies, who dictate the legislation and the execution of the law. The greedy and individualist attitudes of those who retain economic power rule the whole socio-political dynamic, which conveniently favors those in power, who once again reached, maintain, and grow their superiority by oppressing the majority of the population. While the powerful economic minority accumulates larger and larger unmeasurable wealth, which they cannot even utilize, the rest and vast majority of people struggle to survive.

When we all reach higher moral maturity, laws will be unnecessary for us to have social justice and equality.

10

SELF-CARE

When exposed to suffering, losses, and discrimination, from past and present stories of countless people for decades on the clinical psychology career path, overwhelming oppressive feelings are inevitable at times. There are days during which I feel the suffering of political refugees, others the painful traumas experienced by illegal immigrants, sometimes tortured, exploited, and violated while crossing the borders, looking for survival. Other days, I experience the internalized oppression and constant persecution experienced by the black community, persecuted for the "crime" of carrying a larger amount of melanin in their skin. Some days I feel the experience of the indigenous people who had their homes invaded and were violently exterminated by the Europeans during colonial times. The oppression of empathizing with the suffering of others is a constant issue among caregivers and professionals who deal directly with the intimate problems of others.

Neverthless, it is what keeps us alive, bringing purpose and meaning to our lives. Self-care is essential to maintain one's physical and mental health.

Studies show that the constant exposition to a castrating, persecutory, and destructive reality can generate internalized oppression, in which the individual or group internalizes the experienced reality consecutively and repeatedly, and this leads him/her to divest him/herself of freedom, happiness and success, even when his/her external reality enables him/her. The saddest is the fact that those internalized feelings can be passed from generation to generation.

As a remedial measure, I brought the laptop to the backyard, being able to refresh my energies by a majestic elm tree. It reminds me of the trees from my maternal grandmother's backyard, even more attractive due to its delicious tropical fruits. Nothing is more refreshing then the contact with nature. As the harmony between people in our planet, it is equally important for us to re-establish our connection with nature. Such reconnection is the key to health and well-being of all, individually and collectively, as we are all part of the same ecosystem.

11

A ROLE MODEL
AND A HERO

Once there was a boy who didn't know how to walk. Past three years of age, his development progressed normally in all the other milestones. But he didn't walk. This was a source of concern for the whole family. At that time there was no access to paramedic treatments, or even regular visits to a pediatrician due to the distance. Herbal medication and diet were the main resources for good health. His mother and older siblings used to talk to him, giving him encouragement and at times even losing their patience, getting frustrated with the attempts to help him walk. The extended family would say that he wouldn't walk because he was spoiled by his older sisters. As the baby of the family, overwhelmed by their loving care, carrying him up and down everywhere in super funny and comfortable arms and shoulder rides, he didn't have any real reason to walk by himself, losing all that fun and attention.

During one of his Saturday visits, his uncle and godfather, who had so much affection and love for that little boy, observing that his godson did not appear to have any physical or mental disability, and had in fact all the physiological and neurological resources to walk normally, made him an offer: "If next time I come to visit you here you are walking like a big boy, I will give you one "tostão"[1] (the monetary unit of that time period in Brazil).

The caring uncle and godfather gave his farewells with big hugs and a smell on him holding his beloved nephew in his arms. The following Monday, the godfather returned and was greeted by the little boy walking perfectly, coming in his direction with open arms. The uncle radiant and very happy, honored his promise and passed the money to the boy, satisfied to finally confirm that the boy indeed was perfectly normal. In other words, the assumptions of the whole family were correct, that was just a matter of lack of motivation. It could also very well be caused by the trauma of losing his father at a very young age, cured by the presence of another positive male figure as his uncle and godfather in his life. He kept being the beloved and well-cared-for baby to his mother and sisters.

And that is the start of the saga of a man whose life revolved around multiple lessons of growing and

---

1   Real, plural reis, was the currency during the colonial times in Brazil and after the independence from Portugal until 1942, when it was replaced by the cruzeiro. A tostão corresponded to 100 reis.

development, which not by coincidence, were many times related to money. With a heart filled with dreams and wishes of prosperity but also compassion and caring toward everyone around him, at the age of twelve, the young Antonio, already started to work, by his own initiative, helping his mother at her farm and the neighbors at the festive town of Caruarú, state of Pernambuco, Brazil. The country life, living on the land left by his deceased father, was not at all appealing to him. His passions and aspirations, since childhood, involved elegant designer clothing, fancy cars, valuable watches, collections of leather shoes, formally polished, sophisticated houses and the busy social life of the city.

At the age of seventeen , having his older half brother married and out of the house, he decided to move to the capital, Recife, to work with a family friend, Mr. Domingos. His work employment contract said: "apprentice to shoe artisan." In fact making shoes was an art back then. To prepare the leather, to create the models, to calculate the proportions, to make the different pieces and assemble them all, set his artistic and mathematical talents on fire, two of his biggest fortes. Some time later, he was ready to open his own shoe factory. In that town he also met the love of his life, to whom he got married. In a few years, he reached some financial stability, enough to bring his mother and young sister to live at the capital with him. His dreams of prosperity and good living never overcame his good, generous heart, always protecting and providing for his loved ones.

He took over the responsibility of being the head of the family. His mother was a wise woman, well-known and respected by everyone who knew her in town, for her skills as a midwife and professional baker. She didn't put this role on him, but it was his nature to be a caregiver and provider. To some, it would seem pure male chauvinism, but those who knew him were sure that was a matter of pure and legitimate kindness and care for those he loved.

His innate panache for numbers and business, allied with a tireless will and professional enthusiasm, made him prosper. He could expand his empire in Recife, a well developed and prosperous city, plenty of archeological and historical heritage, being the first capital of the country.

The northeast of Brazil carries one of the most ancient archeological sites of the country, dating to more than 40,000 years ago. Recife made his presence also in the pre-Cabralian development of Brazil. The theories about who was the first European to set foot in the lands now called Brazil are controversial. The most accepted states the Spanish Vicent Yanes Pinzon by January 26, 1500, possibly at the St. Agostine Cape, on south shore of Pernambuco. The place seen by Pinzon was always surrounded by controversy. To some Portuguese researchers, like Duarte Leite, the Spanish disembarked north from Orange Cape, at the current French Guiana. But for their castelhano opponents, who based their statements on Pizon's stories, the landing took place at St. Agostine, eighty-six days before the arrival pf Pedro Alvares Cabral to Porto Seguro, state of Bahia. A legal dispute succeeded after Pizon's trip, called Probanzas del Fiscal, a balloting move by Diego Colombo, Cristopher Colombo's son, against the Castela's crown, to secure his father's rights. By 1501, the year after the arrival of the Portuguese in Brazil, the territory of Pernambuco, defined by the Tordesilhas Treaty as a region belonging to Portuguese America, was exploited by the expedition of Gaspar de Lemos, who had created betterments along the colonial coast, possibly including the present locality of Igarassu, trusted later to Cristovão Jacques.

The effective settlement of Pernambuco, however, was initiated around 1534, when a Portuguese colony was divided into heritage captaincies. The territory of the current state of Pernambuco, donated to Duarte Coelho and part of the captaincies of Itamaracá, donated to Pero Lopes de Sousa, extended for sixty leagues between the Iguaraçú river and St. Francisco river.

In 1535, Duarte Coelho took possession of the captaincy, initially baptized by "New Lusitania", but shortly after, it was given its current name. The settlements of Igarassú and Olinda, established in 1535, with the arrival of the donor, were graduated to ville in 1537.

The Pernambuco captaincy embraced the current states of Pernambuco, Paraíba, Rio Grande do Norte,

Ceará and Alagoas as well as the eastern portion of Bahia. Pernambuco was the richest captaincy of the colonial Brazil. Olinda was given the status of administrative capital and its haven, inhabited by fishermen, gave birth to the city of Recife.

The rich history, the economic and cultural development of the region did not seem to be enough for Antonio, the dreamer and entrepreneur. In 1950, after five years of marriage and three children, his next adventure toward Rio de Janeiro started. From the colonial times to the 1950s, much has happened in Brazil. The southeast of the country has taken the lead in national development; Rio de Janeiro became the capital of the country for a while and a brand-new city, Brasilia, had been built from blueprints up, to become the new federal capital district of Brazil in the central west. The southeast nevertheless retains top priority on the economic and cultural center stage, thanks to new waves of immigrants from Japan, Italy, Spain, Germany, Poland, Croatia, Russia, Saudi Arabia, Palestine, Syria, Lebanon, and Israel. These immigrants ranged from political and religious refugees, running from persecution and the devastating economic crisis in Europe and Asia at that time, after the two world wars and Nazi persecutions to people looking for a better life and freedom. So, there went Antonio, reaching new frontiers, well attuned to the optimism of the golden years. He moved on first to get established, providing new housing for the family, and going back a few months later to

Recife to bring the whole family with him. In fact, Rio de Janeiro did not disappoint him. His shoe factory prospered, he purchased new real estate and a small farm for vacations, made numerous new friends and had four more children, including myself. Everywhere he went, his extroverted personality, talkative behavior, and kind heart, always ready to help close ones and strangers alike, offering them shelter, food, jobs, and moral support, gained the friendship and appreciation of many. Our home was always full of people and every day seemed like a holiday party.

But then a great deception came unexpectedly. His then trusted business partner created a huge deficit in the company's budget and disappeared. The heartbreak of working so hard to achieve wealth without anybody's help, of helping so many people for pure charity and still being the victim of such disgraceful attitude, was too hard of a reality for any human to endure. He was back to square one. After a couple of months, he found enough inner strength to get up from his deep depression that such egregious circumstances had triggered and started to search for alternatives to restart. The burden of his debts was such that he had to sell all his assets in order to pay them all. With deep pain and disenchantment, he moved on.

Past such traumatic incidents, Rio de Janeiro now seemed to be full of bad memories, and carried a bitter taste. São Paulo would be the most realistically viable alternative, considering the circumstances. Endowed with the courage, vivacity, and initiative peculiar to him, there goes the middle-aged Antonio, no longer as euphoric and optimistic about his future as he once had been, toward the economic and cultural capital of Brazil. The same way, he continued, re-stablished himself, got a house for the family and a few months later, went back to Rio to bring the whole family. Only this time, the story was much more complex. His older children, already teenagers, suffered the separation from friends, and life in São Paulo brought him some family challenges. As a religious man, feeling the pressure imposed by the ecclesiastical environment to keep his kids in church, Antonio suffered much by seeing most of his older kids, now rebellious teenagers and youth, refusing to go to church, starting to get involved in the hippie movements, buying super fast cars and getting into accidents. The sons now had long '60s hair, platform shoes, and bell-bottom pants. One middle daughter was dating, wearing mini skirts, and even smoking cigarettes. The guilt certainly hunted him for decades, without being able to accept that in fact he didn't have a choice and that was the destiny for all of us.

When I started to understand things, around three and half years of age, we moved to São Paulo and this more chaotic family was what I remember. My father was irritated by problems at work and at home, closed and fearful of new dreams and disillusionment. However, soon he conquered again his financial stability, acquired new real estate, beach houses, land, and new cars. His children all got settled behaviorally and emotionally and became good, well-adjusted, moral, lawful, and productive people, each in their own way. Even the difficulties of life, pain and disappointments did not harden his heart for the needs of the less fortunate, and our house remained full of friends and extended family who asked for his help. As always, he offered them shelter, financial support, and jobs in his company. Also his hardships did not impact his spontaneity and generosity with all, creating new countless friends. He built a dignified, honest life, and became an example of resilience, faith, kindness, and courage, not only to me and my siblings, but to all who had the privilege to know him. He received honorary prizes from São Paulo's Chamber of Commerce, and from his church for decades of community service, and from those who reached him from everywhere.

His history may not seem relevant to the experiences of international immigrants. However, having observed my parents' trajectory, migrating from city to city, estate to estate, from the northeast to the southeast of Brazil, the cultural shocks and stigmas, their impact on one's self-esteem, adjustment, and mental health were very similar to those who migrate internationally. Even the language, with its idiosyncrasies, different accents, idiomatic expressions, body language, moral, and behavior codes, and gender roles are distinctly different from one region to another in large countries like Brazil and the USA. My father, even though he never had wished to leave his country, was the typical immigrant, trailblazing, and groundbreaking new horizons in search for a better life. Nevertheless, he provided me with a solid foundation, financing and supporting my academic development, and yet being a shinning example of kindness, unconditional love, altruism, generosity, vivacity, courage, and resilience.

Having personally experienced the painful challenges of the immigration process on multiple occasions, my plans to come to the USA did not sound like a good idea to him. Initially, I would come only for two years to get a master's degree at New York University. But when things changed and I decided to live here, even when not yet adjusted, he broke into inconsolable weeping, in private conversation with my youngest brother. Now I understand why. He knew what waited for me, how much such a journey would cost me emotionally, taking my floor away at times and compelling me to build a totally new reality from the ground up. Being far away, he could not give me the support and care he would like.

Now, from the other side of the rainbow, I know he also understands how much that made me grow, how much stronger and wiser I became for learning the only truth of our existence: that we are all voyagers. Even when one does not feel as such, when one lives, gets old, and dies at the same geographic familiar location, giving the illusion of living at his/her home, even then one is a voyager, as we all are. Life is a volatile and rapid passage, where nothing is permanent and nothing is guaranteed. To awaken to this reality, and to learn how to deal with it, is the greatest treasure one can acquire. It helped me to value time with responsibility, giving up the vanities of the soul. I learned to value those who love me, loving them and accepting them with all my heart, yet valuing happiness, self-care, and dignity. I learned how to understand the pain of loss, and the importance of the here and now. I had to learn how to use my own wings, yet still keep myself grounded. I learned to believe in my own strengths, to find the transforming power of unconditional optimism, under any circumstances. These were all lessons which I probably would not have learned if not for those experiences.

In his book *Man's Search for Meaning,* Viktor Frankl writes the true story of his experiences as a prisoner for three years in a Nazi camp. He found and experienced the same antidote to the poison of identity loss. In the cases of the Holocaust victims, absolutely nothing was preserved from their lives and dignity. Yet some, like him, conquered inner forces which they never dreamed of pursuing, using each crumb of happiness, created by their own brave and heroic minds, so they could maintain their bodies alive during the most outrageous reality. What is the explanation of how one can survive for three or more years with a small portion of watery soup and a single miserable slice of bread a day, taken in dirty bowls and hands, after long days of forced physical labor in open air, through frozen winters, without shoes or appropriate clothing, without a break, sleeping in dirty and cold accommodations along with rats and other pests, without showers or clean clothes, pilled up together like discarded objects in a trash dump? How can we understand the resistance of their immune systems in constant war against ferocious micro and macroscopic enemies, being attacked on physical, environmental, social and psychological levels, without even minimal nutrition? Those who made it could rely only on the self-sustaining nourishing of their souls on optimism and hope.

Such a phenomenon proves that it is possible to overcome the vast majority of circumstances, sometimes considered unbearable, if we believe. The human mind, when in alignment with one's existential essence and the laws of nature, is capable of feats that can be described as miraculous. From recovery of terminal diseases and serious traumas, people reach their cure in the strength of their own souls. Mainstream science still can find no basis to explain that.

Similarly, we can rewrite our own history, starting from scratch if necessary, after total loss, including our own identity. This is, without a doubt, the most important legacy that my father and ancestral immigrants left to me, and in my turn I leave it to my daughter and to all of you who read this book.

12

WRAPPING UP

After a very hard day reflecting upon circumstances and difficult decisions to be made, I was pleasantly surprised by a pat on the shoulder by a dear friend of mine, who was once my co-worker and is also one of my good neighbors. Always with a polite and sweet attitude typical of him, this Caucasian middle-aged man insisted that I should take his place in the line of the supermarket. The conversation was pleasant and light, bringing the right amount of softness to a difficult day. I then thought about the sense of community I now feel in my town and state, remarkably different from when I moved to this country almost two decades ago. Suddenly, the background music on the radio switched to one of the first hits of the band The Back Street Boys, which for some reason became very meaningfully attached to my process of moving to the Unites States back in the late '90s. Amazingly, this song had not been played in the radio for a long time, but coincidently was on right at that moment of re-signifying and redirecting many things in my life.

On my way home, it made me think about many things I have experienced throughout those years in America: the cooperative closeness with community leaders, working in partnership with the Brazilian consulate, American senators, deputy, law enforcement personal, city councils, chambers of commerce, non-profit organizations. Feeling grateful for being able to contribute to the improvement of people's lives in many levels, both born Americans and immigrants. I also recalled my experiences in music, the opera performances in Boston, with all those interesting groups, all the friends I gathered through those experiences--some dear ones are already deceased, but they left great positive impressions on my personal journey. It also made me recall an American opera I came across lately called *The Consul* by Gian Carlo Menotti. I am currently studying the soprano aria titled "To This We've Come.":

(…) That men withhold the world from men.
(…) That man be born a stranger upon God's earth,
(…) This is my answer: My name is woman, Age: still Young, (…)
Color of eyes: the color of tears, Occupation: Waiting; Waiting; Waiting.

I am waiting, and working, for the day when we all can join in celebration of our differences and the diversity that made us strong as a species! This is a celebration which, in its turn, will make us strong as a planet!

CONCLUSION

Immigration has multiple and complex aspects, which are interrelated and interdependent. As with every social phenomena, its meaning, desirability, value, judgement of the fact in itself as well as the individuals and groups involved one way or the other, radically change depending on the historical, social and economic contexts or the perspective in which its analyzed.

Most of the time, amplifying our views by learning and understanding things through historical and scientific data is of great importance in helping us not to be taken by the alienating and manipulative agendas of our present economic and political reality. By the 1600s, the arrival of the first Europeans from England to the USA, as well as the arrival of the Spanish and Portuguese to Central and South America, were the source of genocide and devastation to the native indigenous people, living in those territories. In the mid-20th century, the massive Italian and Irish immigration to the USA was taken as a threat to American social and economic stability. Most locals treated them with segregation and prejudice, failing to see the obvious causes of such need – particularly World War II, to which the USA heavily contributed, devastating mostly European and Asian territories, destroying their economy, infrastructure, families, and social stability. The current massive immigration movements to the USA from Latin America are perceived with the same shallow, prejudice response from the American community, who in fact is likewise oblivious to the manipulation of the political-economic interests behind the cause of such movement (the globalization of the world's economy, which is beneficial only to the economic oligarchies), the prejudice (as it gives other economic oligarchies the alibi to cash massive sums of trillionaire profits over the incarceration industries), and immigration itself (the double standards, which allow corporations to freely cross international frontiers, destroying local economies, but do not allow the victims of this destruction to reach for survival). The immigrants are the victims and scapegoats of this predatory economy, the ones who are guaranteeing the occupancy of the lucrative jail beds and tremendous growth of the incarceration industry, but yet being portrayed as a danger and threat.

Taking all this into consideration, the understanding of and the approaches to deal with immigration, both in social and in individual contexts, should be also wide and panoramic. Solutions need to be found by harmonizing a wide variety of aspects in order to achieve a more objective view, and therefore a more positive outcome.

From the psychological point of view, under social, collective, or individual realms, immigration must likewise be understood and dealt within a holistic manner. Both the individual and the collective are immersed in a vast array of historical, economic, political, cognitive, emotional, and physical factors, which play important roles, both separately and in association among themselves, to contribute to the immigration reality of our times.

Therefore, it would be vain and foolish to treat the immigrant as an isolated entity, completely detached from global, historical, economic, political, and collective contexts. Contrary to what is promoted by the media, the immigrant is not someone who has chosen to break rules deliberately or to cause disturbances in the local and international order; seeing immigrants as the cause of the social and economic problems the locals are facing is a major ignorance. The alienated and individualistic way of living of most people, failing to acknowledge the effects that our intentions, choices, and actions (or inactions) have on one another is a mistake that creates most of our personal and social issues.

From a clinical perspective, both in individual and group contexts, this awareness and the appropriate changes consistent with this broader and holistic understanding are the most effective approach to treat any disorder, including the issues related to immigration. For the immigrant, awareness of and removal of guilt from his/her circumstance and social role, are the first steps to rebuild self-esteem, identity, and consequently psychological and physiological health. For the non-immigrant prejudiced citizen, a panoramic awareness of their own immigrant background, as well as an understanding of the social, economic, and political contexts in which immigration occurs will help them and our society to function with healthier standards.

All the negative repercussions of the immigration and acculturation processes are heavily related to the prejudice against the immigrants and the consequent obstacles toward social and psychological adjustments. The unfairness, segregation, and discrimination with which the immigrant is treated by all levels of society, from law enforcement, to the justice system, to work-related matters, to daily personal and social relationships, create an inhuman, unhealthy, and destabilizing atmosphere that leads to all sorts of mental, physical, and social imbalances. If not for that brutal, destructive negative reaction against them, all the initial adjustments would be experienced and surpassed fairly easily, just like any adaptation our species is equipped to reach--which, by the way, we have conquered in the past since prehistoric times.

The receiving countries, for the most part, conveniently "forget" their contribution to the overall international issues behind immigration needs. As if the losses and risks the immigrants need to face by leaving their culture and the comfort of their natural habitat were not enough, they become once again the victims of being the villains in history. This experience is similar to the objectification and desensitization of women's issues, for example, the rape, in which the woman, victim of rape, is judged as responsible for the barbaric and sociopathic advances of the rapist, just for looking attractive or for not being careful enough; it also mirrors the stereotypes given to the the black community as being violent or criminally inclined, when in fact they are the victims of centuries of crimes, injustice, and violence against them, being brutally attacked at all levels of society, solely due to the color of their skin. If, God forbid, they react in self- defense against police brutality or uncalled-for unjust judgments, this is only added to the arguments against them.

It's about time for us to change the broken record of humanity, of gaining from other's losses, oppressing the already oppressed, taking advantage of the weak, villainizing the victims and glorifying the predators. Until then, we will all continue to walk toward self-destruction as a human race and as a planet.

Collectively speaking, since the emergence of the primates, especially *Homo sapiens*, much knowledge has achieved and accumulated through time: from the erect and upright gait to spaceships; from the discovery of the fire to atomic missiles; from the verbal communication to quantum physics; from small primate groups to multinational market managements. Besides what we have today, many technologically and scientifically advanced civilizations were destroyed through natural disasters or for unknown reasons in the past, and with them went all their accumulated knowledge.

Meanwhile, the moral evolution of our species advanced a few timid steps, compared to the growth of our cognition, neurobiological capacities, and technology. From ancient civilizations to now, the Egyptians, Persians, Romans, Greeks, Portuguese, Spanish, British, French, Germans, Russians, and Americans, very little achievements were made in the direction of sustainable knowledge, production, economy, and sociopolitical systems. Individualistic, competitive, destructive, and aggressive conduct and perspectives are the basis of our "civilized" world as much as they were for the Neanderthals, except for technological advancements. The brutality and savagery only gained a different appearance, through ideological manipulations and justifications, institucionalizations, or even through hypocritical dissimulations. The sociopathies hide behind social, institutional, and corporate structures, in order to manipulate the attempts toward moral progress represented by constitutional legal articles, in search of social justice, equality, human rights and ecological responsibilities. Instead of following them and ensuring their enforcement in a fair and egalitarian way, laws are used as domineering and oppressive instruments against the less privileged.

Through history, power has circulated through diverse formats. Dynasties, political, religious, and ideological oligarchies, totalitarianism, democracies, socialisms, capitalism; the ideologies, as well as social, political, and economic systems are all transformed, replacing one another--maintaining however, the basic essence: domination, competition, and oppression. Lapses of systems morally more developed are observed here and there, but as a culture, we are still very underdeveloped, living in brutal and unintelligent moral patterns.

Regardless of leading-edge technologies, which allow us to see, measure, and analyze from Higgs-Boson particles to intergalactic spaces, we fail to see the obvious correlation between our intentions, thoughts, and feelings with the creation of the chaos in which we live, socially and collectively.

Advances in quantum physics show in mathematical and experimental terms the interrelation between material and virtual realities, uncovering the energetic nature of the center of the atom and therefore, everything that exists in the universe. It shows also the energetic and energy-generating nature of thoughts and feelings, through mathematical formulas and experiments, measuring those energy waves, directions, and intensity, which are capable of altering and creating what before was understood as matter. None of this is worth anything if we fail in our ability to understand the obvious implications of such advancements, inter-connecting matter to energy, body and spirit, science and spirituality, cognition and morality. We must act on obvious understanding that harmonic intentions and thoughts will create a harmonious world, and only this way will our personal and collective achieve-ments and advancements be sustainable. We must take to heart the obvious understanding that if one single cancerous cell is capable of multiplying and destroying the whole organism, then in the same way, individual-istic, competitive and antisocial attitudes are destruc-tive to the whole social system into which every single individual is inserted. Choosing and leading a non-altruistic and compassionless life, therefore, consists of the most ignorant, intellectually deprived, and self-de-structive attitude, failing to understand that from the greedy corporate oligarchies to the simple citizen, we all have the same responsibility on the chaotic outcome we experience today.

Like primates, humanity still engages in territo-rial disputes and leadership conquests through force, alienation, and destruction of the opponent. The in-satiable thirst for power and the infinite accumulation of wealth became a lethal vice, which is destroying not only our species but also Planet Earth.

The immigration phenomenon needs to be under-stood through a panoramic view. Why do individu-als migrate from one place to another? Which factors determine the emergence of such needs? What are the historical perspectives of the migratory phenomena since the beginning of humanity? What are the truly effective solutions for the problems causing and caused by the migratory movements in each historical moment, as well as within a trans-historical perspective?

If we step aside to a wider view, we can observe the recurrence of such phenomena throughout human history. The translocation and exploration of new habitats consist is one of the main differentiating aspects of the human species in relation to others, bringing us to a privileged position in our eco-system. By migrating, *Homo sapiens* conquered adaptative and evolutionary advantages and therefore tremendous guarantees to perpetuate our species. Thanks to immigration, humanity acquired the adaptative characteristics that this movement promoted, which were essential to enable us to survive in all and each region of the globe.

The racial and ethnic diversities, which today are an object of segregation, prejudice, competition, exploitation, rivalries, and disputes, are nothing more than an adaptive mechanism, which granted and still enable the survival of our species, all over the planet as well as our evolutionary leadership position in nature.

While we act as fools, rejecting our differences, we all should join in celebrating them, as they are what enabled the existence of each one of us, without exception, to this day. Without diversity, which was conquered throughout eras and millennia of different migratory movements all over the planet, our species would have already reached extinction, as many others did.

Nevertheless, more important than the microscopic analysis is the conclusive finding that, if we evolve to more elevated moral levels, living naturally and in egalitarian and just social organizations, based on the awareness that the individual's well-being and preservation intrinsically depends on the common good, we would not be facing what, today, we consider the causative factors or problems related to immigration. A peaceful, cooperative, co-responsible and respectful co-existence among all, toward one another and nature, would create a reality free of the imbalances that today generate social conflicts, and survival threats to individuals and the collective.

For some, such a concept seems an unreachable utopia, magical thinking, a childish fantasy. However, quantum physics and positive psychology have proven it is not. Those who allow themselves to experience personal and environmental transformations through the understanding and practice of such principles, are able to verify its veracity and accessibility to all. It is not a matter of faith or suggestible ideology; it is physics, as real as the light, the changes in temperatures, the forces of gravity, or any other physical phenomena.

If we believe and practice every day a lifestyle based on self-acceptance and love and acceptance for others, as well as peace and harmony among people throughout our planet, we can create this reality for ourselves. If a cancer can be cured by a positive attitude and the will-power of the individual and their loved ones, the cancers of our societies can likewise be eradicated by the changes cultivated inside of each one of us.

God bless America as a whole, not only the economic oligarchies. God bless our planet, bringing peace and harmony to all people and nature. Without peace among people and responsible coexistence with nature, there will be no Planet Earth and therefore no America tomorrow. Regardless of whether we acknowledge it or not, we are one of many interdependent parts on this huge and complex system called Planet Earth and the universe.

Natives, foreigners, blacks, whites, rich, poor, oligarchies, proletariat, capitalists, and socialists—all labels are pointless to understand and to solve the core of our social and environmental problems. We are all in this together!

BIBLIOGRAPHY

1- Scudder, Samuel H.; William M. Davis; Charles W. Woodworth; Leland O. Howard; Charles V. Riley; Samuel W. Williston (1989). The Butterflies of the Eastern United States and Canada with special reference to New England. The author. p. 721. Retrieved 2008-06-04.

2- Garber, Steven D. (1998). The Urban Naturalist. Courier Dover Publications. pp. 76–79. Retrieved 2008-05-26.

3- Groth, Jacob (November 10, 2000)."Monarch Migration Study." Swallowtail Farms. Retrieved July 21, 2014.

4- "Monarch Migration." Monarch Joint Venture. 2013.

5- James A. Scott (1986). *The Butterflies of North America*. Stanford University Press, Stanford, CA.

6- Chun, Kevin M Chun; Organista, Pamela B.; Matin, Gerardo – " Acculturation- Advances in Theory, Measurement and Applied Research- American Psychological Association- 2002

7- Berry, John; Portinga, Seger M.; Chasiotis, Athanasios; Sam, David L. - "Cross-Cultural Psychology"

8- Pearce Stewart – *"The Alchemy of the Voice."* Findhorn Press. 2005

9- Harris, Roy. *Landmarks in Linguistic Thought 1: The Western Tradition from Socrates to Saussure* -Psychology Press, 1989

10- Michael Tomasello. *Origin of Human Communication.* MIT Press, 2008

11- Tierno Jr, Philip. *The Secret Life of Germs"*- Pocket Books, NY, 2001

12- United States Department of Labor- Bureau of Labor Statistics

13- Migration Policy Institute

14- The American Immigration Council

15- The Center for American Progress Bentley, Jerry H., ed. *The Oxford Handbook of World History* (Oxford University Press, 2011)

16- Bentley, Jerry H. *Shapes of World History in Twentieth Century Scholarship. Essays on Global and Comparative History Series.* (1996)

17- Costello, Paul. *World Historians and Their Goals: Twentieth-Century Answers to Modernism* (1993).

18- Curtin, Philip D. "Depth, Span, and Relevance," *The American Historical Review,* Vol. 89, No. 1 (Feb., 1984), pp. 1–9

19- Dunn, Ross E., ed. *The New World History: A Teacher's Companion.* (2000).

20- Frye, Northrop. "Spengler Revisited" in *Northrop Frye on modern culture* (2003), pp 297–382, first published 1974;

21- * Hare, J. Laurence, and Jack Wells. "Promising the World: Surveys, Curricula, and the Challenge of Global History," *History Teacher*, 48 (Feb. 2015) pp: 371-88.

22- Hughes-Warrington, Marnie. *Palgrave Advances in World Histories* (2005), 256pp, articles by scholars

23- Lang, Michael. "Globalization and Global History in Toynbee," *Journal of World History* 22#4 Dec. 2011 pp. 747–783

24- McInnes, Neil. "The Great Doomsayer: Oswald Spengler Reconsidered." *National Interest* 1997 (48): 65–76.

25- McNeill, William H. "The Changing Shape of World History." *History and Theory* 1995

26- Encyclopædia Britannica, Inc., 1994-2009

27- MARGOLIS, Maxine. *Little Brazil: imigrantes brasileiros em Nova York. Campinas: Papirus, 1994.*

28- NEPO (Núcleo de Estudos de População). *Base de dados bibliográfica sobre imigrantes brasileiros no exterior.* Campinas: Unicamp, 1996.

www.ingramcontent.com/pod-product-compliance
Lightning Source LLC
Chambersburg PA
CBHW070005300526
45794CB00001B/200